MW00366070

VITAL SIGNS

Register This New Book

Benefits of Registering*

- ✓ FREE **replacements** of lost or damaged books
- ✓ FREE **audiobook** – *Pilgrim's Progress,* audiobook edition
- ✓ FREE information about new titles and other **freebies**

www.anekopress.com/new-book-registration

*See our website for requirements and limitations.

VITAL SIGNS

SIGNS

KEYS FOR PERSONAL
AND SPIRITUAL CPR

PHIL AND KELI WADE
FOREWORD BY STEVE DRAKE

ANEKO
PRESS

We love hearing from our readers. Please contact us
at www.anekopress.com/questions-comments with
any questions, comments, or suggestions.

www.philwade.net
Vital Signs
© 2020 by Phil and Keli Wade
All rights reserved. Published 2020.

No part of this book may be reproduced, stored in a retrieval system, or
transmitted in any form or by any means – electronic, mechanical, photocopying,
recording, or otherwise, without written permission from the publisher.

Scripture taken from the New King James Version®. Copyright © 1982
by Thomas Nelson. Used by permission. All rights reserved.
Scripture quotations marked (NIV) are taken from the Holy Bible, New
International Version®, NIV®. Copyright © 1973, 1978, 1984, 2011 by Biblica,
Inc.® Used by permission of Zondervan. All rights reserved worldwide. www.
zondervan.com The "NIV" and "New International Version" are trademarks
registered in the United States Patent and Trademark Office by Biblica, Inc.®

Cover Design: Jonathan Lewis

Printed in the United States of America
Aneko Press
www.anekopress.com
Aneko Press, Life Sentence Publishing, and our logos are trademarks of
Life Sentence Publishing, Inc.
203 E. Birch Street
P.O. Box 652
Abbotsford, WI 54405
RELIGION / Christian Living / Spiritual Growth
Paperback ISBN: 978-1-62245-674-1
eBook ISBN: 978-1-62245-675-8
10 9 8 7 6 5 4 3 2 1
Available where books are sold

Contents

DEDICATION

This book is dedicated first to my Lord Jesus Christ for redeeming that which was lost and broken.

Next, to my wife, Keli, for staying with me out of obedience to God when I know your flesh told you to run. The journey together has been crazy, but your godly beauty and character have been vital in keeping me on track. My story would be incomplete without you. You are the love of my life!

Then to my children and their spouses, Brian, Katie, Maridith, and Robert, who give me reason to stay in the race. You challenge me and encourage me with passion to live beyond the normal. You are my heroes.

To my grandchildren, Anniston, Roman, Shepherd, Roscoe, and Neyland. I have written this book that you may know that God can take the most broken of vessels and use them for His glory. May your plans be His plans, and may you never ever cave to the ways of the world. It is vital that you aggressively pursue intimacy with Jesus more than anything.

To my brothers, Andy and Danny. Thank you for loving me in spite of my rebellion and never quitting on me. To watch you live your lives is to watch Jesus in action. You are my heroes.

To my mom, Judi Wade. Watching you have both knees

replaced, I am reminded that it was probably the overtime you spent praying for me that wore them out. It is, without any doubt, your sweet spirit, your love for me, and your prayers for me that I am what I am today. Thank you for persevering for your prodigal son.

Last, but not least, to my father, Mike Wade. Dad, I wish you were here to hear me preach, to hear Danny sing, to watch Andy continually walk closer to Jesus, to laugh at and with your grandchildren and great-grandchildren, and to watch Mom be who only she can be, even when a piece of her heart is missing: you. I wish you were here to read my story of which you were and still are so much a part. But, please, stay where you are – I will see you soon. I love and miss you.

FOREWORD

And He has made from one blood every nation of men to dwell on all the face of the earth. – Acts 17:26

It is true! All of us from every age, every tribe, and every tongue have a single progenitor. God made us all from that one fountain head, and we are the same family in that regard. However, to a large degree, the similarities stop there. We may be of the same blood, but there is a plethora of personalities, opinions, looks, sounds, hair colors, hair textures, and hair styles. Not to mention there are endless numbers of attitudes and sizes.

Like walking through a pet shelter and seeing all the critters of various descriptions – some barking, some staring, some playing with cage-mates, and others sleeping – one always seems to catch our eye. Each pet is unique, but that one seems somehow to be slightly more unique than the others. That is how I see the author of *Vital Signs*, just a bit more unique than the others.

He comes from the same sea of humanity, all made from one blood, and each unique in his or her own way. Phil Wade has a presence, a demeanor, and an undeniable compassion for others that shines constantly.

He serves as the Lead Pastor for Northside Church in Rome, Georgia. I have attended this church for a year, but my history with Phil numbers just shy of forty years. Phil was one of my first staff acquisitions in my own pastoral ministry. In 1982 Phil accepted a call to the Antioch Baptist Church in Carrollton, Georgia, to be our Minister of Music. Those days have long passed, and our lives have taken different paths, but my love for Phil and his sweet wife, Keli, has never diminished.

Vital Signs is the story of Phil's journey, his challenges in life, his successes and failures, and lessons and victories. Through these events, the author gives keen insights and applications to help others along their journey. The reader will quickly realize how important it is to this author to help others find life, peace, victory, and fullness in their own walk.

Be forewarned, this book has no intention of leaving you as you were when you opened its pages. Its objective is to challenge you to take God at His Word, trust His providence, and rely on His ability to accomplish through you His will. If you will read with a desire to learn and maintain a teachable spirit, you will harvest blessings for you and your tribe for which you will thank this author in years to come.

Stephen Drake, D. Min.

INTRODUCTION

A LIFE BEYOND MEDIOCRITY

Okay, I get it! I know you are thinking, *Here is another one of those the-church-is-in-trouble, we-are-doing-it-all-wrong, and if-you-will-buy-this (program, book, thought, or idea) then everything will become new and old things will pass away.*

That is far from why I wrote this book. My heart is simply to share with you through the journey Christ has had me on for a span of over thirty years of ministry. In the first chapter of this book, we will begin the journey with a look at my story. I hope you will see that if God, the Creator of the universe, can use Phil Wade, as He did a donkey belonging to Balaam, then certainly God can use you to be a miracle-delivering, change agent to bring hope to people who see nothing but hopelessness. God can use you to bring change to those in your circle of influence who are stuck doing life, family, and ministry the way they have always done it, even though it stopped working decades ago. He can use you to bring life back to those faithful followers, servants, leaders, and shepherds who have become weary in doing good.

This journey will include many of my failures, times in

which I thought I was doing well only to discover that I was trying to open the door with the wrong keys.

So, if you are tired of mediocrity, tired of settling for going on half-throttle with little vision and passion that seem to be fading, then welcome aboard.

My goal is to bring about spiritual CPR, cardiopulmonary resuscitation, to every Christ-follower who refuses to settle for mediocrity, desires to finish well, and longs to still be running when the sands of time run out. This book is for every child of God who is willing to dare to dream big and leave behind traditionalism and every weight that stands between his or her reaching that dream.

Someone once said tradition is the "living faith of those who have died" and traditionalism is the "dead faith of those still living." If you dare to choose to deny the latter of the two, step out of the boat, and do some water walking; then, once again, welcome aboard.

If you are like me, you will understand when I tell you that I struggle with getting still and quiet. Often when the Lord reminds me of my need to be still and know that He is God, I reply, *Dad, I get the "You are God" part. However, while I am being still, is there anything I can be doing?* Do not laugh too hard at me, because I know that you know just what I am talking about.

So, since we are so much alike, grab a good cup of hot coffee, your highlighter, pen, and notepad as you settle in to hear what God has to say to you. Let's get this spiritual CPR journey started!

CHAPTER 1

PERSONAL CPR

I will never forget that fateful day in the latter part of the 1980s. My brother Danny, Uncle Tommy, and I were leaving downtown Rome, Georgia, after having lunch, when I spotted a man slumped over the tailgate of a truck. As we drove by, I looked back in time to see him hit the ground. I yelled, "Stop the van!"

My uncle reversed the vehicle so we could go back and assist the elderly man. By the time we reached him, the man was in a full-blown sweat, unconscious, and not breathing. Immediately, we loaded him into the van and began our harrowing trip to Floyd Medical Center, which was only one and a half miles away. Without a doubt, this was the longest mile and a half I have ever traveled. That trip opened my eyes to my inability to help someone needing CPR. I felt as though I was yelling orders at myself, but I was unable to respond – a sort of slow-motion nightmare with slurred speech.

Like someone who is awakened from a bad dream, the sound of emergency room doctors and nurses hustling around us snapped me back to reality. In no time, it seemed, the doctor walked toward us and spoke words that shook me to the core: "I am sorry. He did not make it."

So many questions flooded my mind: *What if I had known CPR? What if we had gotten to him sooner?*

Facing Reality

Consider the relevance of this story as it relates to our experience as believers in Christ. The truth is, as Christ followers and leaders, we will never be able to resuscitate others when we are not able to help ourselves. To reach a position to receive personal CPR requires two things that are of utmost importance:

1. Recognize that we need help.

2. Humble ourselves enough to ask for it.

The Bible speaks to these personal necessities in an account told in the Old Testament:

> *A certain woman of the wives of the sons of the prophets cried out to Elisha, saying, "Your servant my husband is dead, and you know that your servant feared the LORD. And the creditor is coming to take my two sons to be his slaves." So, Elisha said to her, "What shall I do for you? Tell me, what do you have in the house?" And she said, "Your maidservant has nothing in the house but a jar of oil." Then he said, "Go, borrow vessels from everywhere, from all your neighbors – empty vessels; do not gather just a few.* (2 Kings 4:1-3)

Many people today find themselves heartsick because of their own bad choices. Then there are others, much like this woman in the book of Kings, who are in a bad situation not because of anything they have done.

Another account in the Bible speaks to this:

> And they heard the sound of the LORD God walking in the garden in the cool of the day, and Adam and his wife hid themselves from the presence of the LORD God among the trees of the garden. Then the LORD God called to Adam and said to him, "Where are you?" (Genesis 3:8-9)

This was not a question of location, but a question of condition. God knew exactly where they were. He simply wanted them to admit their condition.

When it comes to personal CPR, we must start with the question, what is the spiritual condition of my heart?

Truthfulness in answering this question will determine whether your heart experiences resuscitation so that you can be fully alive in Christ and walk in the freedom God intended for you.

Next Steps

We are not left on our own to figure out how to change. This widow's account provides some practical how-tos:

(1) The first thing we see in the widow's story is her cry of distress. She was hurting so much that she did not struggle to admit she had a problem.

We need to follow her example of being vulnerable and saying we desperately need help – now. Some of us will spend the greater part of our lives in trouble, blaming everyone else or wallowing in shame, rather than humbling ourselves, swallowing our pride, and admitting, "I need help!"

For thirty-plus years of my life, that was how I lived. For example, my anger, which raged to the point of physically abusing my wife, stemmed from an incident in which a man sexually abused me at a young age. I blamed that man for my actions and hid the truth of my past; I desperately needed personal CPR. Yet I never asked for help, much less shared the overpowering pain that consumed my life.

A time must come in everyone's life when the longing to live the abundant life outweighs the pain of our current situation. We need to stop blaming whoever is at fault and start dialing 9-1-1 to get the help we need.

(2) The widow cried to Elisha the prophet, a spiritual leader, a God-fearing man. She did not pursue the psychic hotline or someone in the same mess that she was in.

We must stop looking for advice in all the wrong places. Instead, we must look beyond ourselves and look to God for help.

- We need to take our problems and concerns to God, *casting all your care upon Him, for He cares for you* (1 Peter 5:7).

- Then we need to reach out to our brothers or sisters in Christ who love us enough to get into the trenches with us and tell us the truth. Proverbs 27:17 says, *As iron sharpens iron, so a man sharpens the countenance of his friend.*

As a pastor, I have learned through life-coaching people that it is not about giving the right answers as much as it is helping people find the right answers.

(3) The widow took a step of faith. She explains, *I have nothing except a little jar of oil.* Bingo! Right answer! She had nothing.

Many times God has allowed me to come to this point to show me who I am and where I am in comparison to who He is. Here are the hard facts: We are nothing, and God is everything.

One of my favorite passages that drives this home to me is 1 Chronicles 29:11-12:

> *Yours, O Lord, is the greatness, The power and the glory, The victory, and the majesty; For all that is in heaven and in earth is Yours; Yours is the kingdom, O LORD, And You are exalted as head over all. Both riches and honor come from You, And You reign over all. In your hand is power and might. In Your hand it is to make great, And to give strength to all.*

Desperate Measures

If you are like me in the slightest way, you don't have a problem admitting that you are nothing and God is everything. If that is the case, answer these questions:

- Why is it that we often struggle to go to God when we need His help the most?

- When we fall short of the glory of God, why do we lock ourselves into our own prison cell?

I will tell you why. Shame! Shame causes us to drop our heads and live with no vitality. Satan loves nothing more than shaming us to the point of believing we are unworthy.

We must block out the lies and listen to Jesus, who whispers to us, "I said that I love you unconditionally. I will never leave you nor forsake you. Your past is in your head and your future is in my hands. Rise up, child of mine. It is time for some personal CPR." Just hearing those words gets me excited. However, do not miss the point in the story of the widow when Elisha made it a personal thing. He told the widow *to go*. She had to take a personal step of faith, even if she might look like a fool. Can you imagine going up to your neighbor saying, "Excuse me, the creditors are coming to take my boys as slaves. May I borrow some fruit jars – a bunch of them, please?" However, she had two choices: risk looking like a fool and go for help or lose her sons.

The paradigm shift for this woman was her desperation to keep her boys. As Scripture tells us, her husband died and left some debts unpaid; the creditors were coming to collect payment. If this widow did not come up with the money, these creditors would take her boys as slaves. I believe we can confess that the thought of losing our children would call for desperate measures, even at the risk of looking like a fool by asking for help.

Taking the Plunge

What risks do we need to take to jump-start our hearts afresh and anew? We must stop caring what others might think or say, step out of the boat in faith, and start some water-walking.[1]

The desperate widow did not need a little help. She needed a lot of help. May we follow her example, stop beating around the bush, go boldly before the throne of God, and admit we really need help? I promise God will not be put out with you, nor will He be surprised.

Father, my personal finances need fixing.

Father, my broken heart needs healing.

---

1   Reference to Matthew 14:22-33.

Father, my unwillingness to forgive needs overhauling.

Father, it is not my actual physical heart, but my spiritual/emotional heart that needs renewing.

After you confess your need for God's performing CPR on your heart, wait on Him and trust in Him.

There is more to the widow's story. God was about to take the little oil she had and miraculously multiply it to supply all she needed to save the lives of her sons as well as secure their family's future.

> *"And when you have come in, you shall shut the door behind you and your sons; then pour it into all those vessels and set aside the full ones." So she went from him and shut the door behind her and her sons, who brought the vessels to her; and she poured it out. Now it came to pass, when the vessels were full, that she said to her son, "Bring me another vessel." And he said to her, "There is not another vessel." So, the oil ceased. Then she came and told the man of God. And he said, "Go, sell the oil and pay your debt; and you and your sons live on the rest."* (2 Kings 4:4-7)

Take note of how this passage begins: *When you have come in, shut the door behind you and your sons.* This has now become a teachable moment for her and her sons. The sons witnessed God work a miracle in their mother's life. God was also giving them the opportunity for spiritual renewal in their own hearts as their mother took them along on her spiritual journey.

I will never forget when our daughter, Maridith, came to

us and asked to go to college out of state. Our response was a resounding no due to finances, as her in-state tuition would be covered by state funds. Our answer was not to her liking. As the Christian daughter that she is, she countered with, "If God is in it, He will make a way." Then I, pastor/dad, countered with, "When you and God get it worked out, let me know how it goes."

Weeks later, with a grin of sarcasm, Maridith requested a family meeting at which she explained the plan she and God had put together. God had blessed her willingness to step out in faith. Maridith moved to Andrews, North Carolina, and went to work with Snowbird Wilderness Outfitters. My friends Brody and Little Holloway paid her first-year tuition.

After the first year, she became a resident of North Carolina. Between in-state funding and Snowbird, God had it all worked out. "Dad," Maridith explained, "I was certain the same God that has met every need we had as a family all these years would not have a problem making my dream come true." Wow! What a humbling thing it is to be taught a lesson by your child whom you have taught for years by simply taking them on the journey with you.

Back to the widow woman. Did you notice what God miraculously did?

- As long as the empty vessels kept coming, the oil kept flowing.

- It is true that God can take our little and make much of it if we simply make it available to Him.

Regardless of how much or how little heart we have left to give, we each must make a personal decision to give it back to its rightful owner. If we are going to experience a personal and spiritual CPR, it is vital to remember "little is much when God is in it."

CHAPTER 2

FALSE IDENTITY AND THE UGLY TRUTH

For some of you, your heart beats afresh and anew. For that, we pause to thank God. However, others still struggle to discover who you really are and how you got here. While most of us want to be difference-makers and superheroes for the kingdom, we are often in a category quite different from these. At least, this was true for me.

My Story

In my personal journey to discover who I really was, I learned of many types of individuals. Oh yes, I am sure you have met every one of these at some point in your life as well.

- The arrogant, self-sufficient person who denies all feelings and has no need for the law because he thinks he is the law; he never asks for help and never apologizes.

- The brainless bully who ridicules everyone else to

build himself up. He will not and cannot admit that nobody likes him.

- The colossal coward who is so lacking in confidence that even the neighborhood T-ball team pushes him around.

- Then last, the chameleon who is so confused about who he is that he attempts to blend in with everyone.

Here is where the story gets tough for me. I have walked as each of those at some point in my life.

I was born to Mike and Judy Wade of Knoxville, Tennessee, in August 1962, with an older brother, Andy, and soon to join us, younger brother, Danny. For the most part, we had the look and feel of your typical American family with a hardworking father, who was a great provider and strong disciplinarian. He was so strong in his disciplinary methods that if he parented young children today with the same methods, he'd probably face jail time, if you know what I mean. While I do not promote harsh disciplinary practices, I must confess that it was exactly what I needed to keep me from self-destruction.

Then there is mama Judi. This woman who gave birth to me is a one of a kind. She is fun and gullible; she laughs hysterically, sees the best in everyone, and loves and serves everyone. She is a selfless beauty queen.

Like so many American families of that era, team Wade was in church every Sunday morning and evening as well as every Wednesday night – no excuses or exceptions.

Identity Construction

As an infant in Knoxville, I learned that if I cried loudly when I was hungry, the milk arrived quickly. When I needed a diaper change and let out a good cry, Dad came running, only to gag and pawn me off to good ole Mom. As I continued to grow, I learned how to manipulate and use that cry to get my way. However, it did not take long before my non-gullible dad caught on and informed my mom that I was playing them like a secondhand fiddle.

It is amazing that I had no problem coming up with new ways of getting my selfish desires met at this stage of life. If Mom and Dad would not give in, I reached out to grandparents, siblings, and friends. Before long, they caught on as well, and my being catered to came to a grinding halt. I had to go elsewhere to fulfill my childish desires. Like most boys with unbridled exuberance, I ripped the training wheels off my bike and hit the neighborhood streets. Back then I called it "running away from home."

On one of these disgruntled, run-away-in-the-neighborhood bike rides, two older boys who must have just gotten their driver's licenses confronted me. While joyriding, they spotted me, a little fat kid to bully. They knocked me off my bike and pushed me and my bike into a ditch; they made fun of my big ears and called me fat.

I don't write this to get your sympathy. Rather, I want to bring awareness that in moments like these, many people adopt an identity that they hope will be accepted by all people. We do this because our hearts cannot bear the rejection or that feeling of not fitting in. I understand that this identity is a false identity, but at this point in my life, all I wanted was to fit in. Well, with the humiliation and embarrassment of this belittling, I did what most kids do – I bottled it up and tucked it away.

Secret Me

Soon after this incident our family loaded up the truck and moved to Rome, Georgia, where my father took a sales job in my grandfather's hardware business. Not one for staying indoors, I finally got the nerve to grab my bike and introduce myself to the neighborhood boys in the hope they needed one more riding partner. In the meeting of my new friends, I quickly learned that if I was going to fit in, smoking cigarettes would be part of the deal. The problem with this new cigarette-smoking hobby was that I had no money to buy them, so I stole from my dad and from a small, privately owned store down the street from my house.

While I was stealing a pack of cigarettes from this store one day, the owner caught me. He yelled at me for taking what was not mine and then called me over to him. His voice calmed down as he explained everything that could happen as a result of my stealing. It ranged from his whipping me to calling my dad or even the police.

"Is that what you want son?" he asked with his deep, threatening voice.

With no time needed to think about my reply and with tears in my eyes, I replied, "No sir, please don't get me in trouble."

What followed those words changed my life.

"Son, I won't tell on you and you won't tell on me." With that said, this man had his way with me sexually.

Shattered

Eleven years old, bullied, and sexually abused, I was now on a course to constructing a false identity that would stay with me thirty years down the road. I had so much shame, embarrassment, hurt, and anger, but I told no one.

My life during my teenage years was just north of hell itself. Thoughts of suicide often plagued me. I fought constantly at school and was often suspended. I was in constant pursuit of anything to cover up the pain. My dependence on drugs and alcohol led to almost daily altercations with my dad, while my mom and brothers could only sit, watch, and cry about all the hell I brought to my family. Remember, I had never once told anyone about what had happened to me at the hands of the store owner.

In the middle of one of our fights, my father asked me what I planned to do with my life. My response was that I was going to marry my girlfriend after graduation, move as far away as possible, and never come back. His reply was, "I'll hold you to it."

His response festered in my heart for quite some time, and added fuel to an already rebellious spirit. It is sad when I think about the tragic cycle that played out in my life, and I have seen played out in the lives of so many other young people:

- We get hurt and then begin to hurt others.

- We attempt to run from our problems.

- While running away, we take our problems with us, because we are often the problem.

The Girlfriend

As for the girlfriend to whom I referred in that argument with my dad, meet Keli Bates.

It was 1979. As I sat with my friend Greg Palmer, I gazed across Coosa High School's gym at the most beautiful girl I had ever seen. Without warning, my mouth flew open and out came the words, "Greg, will you go over there and tell Keli Bates that I'm going to marry her?"

So, Greg got up and walked over. Upon his return he said, "Phil, Keli mentioned that you guys might want to date first."

Well, we did, and then I made good on my promise. When we announced our plans to marry to my parents, my mom's words to Keli were, "If you marry Phil Wade, you are a fool! You will be divorced in six months." Keli and I were married on April 18, 1981. I was eighteen years old and Keli was nineteen.

Yes, I will give it to my mom. She had every reason to feel this way after all the anger and rebellion I had unleashed on my family.

If only I knew then what I know now:

- Satan's attempts to derail us are not because of our past.

- Satan uses our past to derail our future.

Because of the blows that life had dealt me, I believed I was worthless, dirty, and unlovable. In my mind, my life had so little value that suicide did not seem that far-fetched. When you are treated as worthless and then told you are worthless, it becomes easier each day to add one more worthless brick to your already constructed false identity.

As a result, I dragged my wife and children through complete hell for years. Before we tear down this false identity, I would like you to hear what it is like to live with someone so busy covering up who he really is that he has no time to help you be all you can be.

As I wrote in the previous chapter, not once in either instance of being bullied or sexually abused, did I ever tell anyone. Well, the ugly truth began to reveal itself with a tough question in a difficult season of our marriage. She says I never tell the story the way it happened. So here is Keli's perspective. Take it away, Babe.

The Ugly Truth – From Keli's Perspective

Perception is everything when one begins to share his or her view on how a given situation took place. A life-changing event can take place between two people and produce two different responses based on the perception of the individual recalling what happened. I personally call this "my footnote moment."

Okay, go ahead and take a deep breath. Now release it. Dive in as I allow you to join me on this journey of discovering the ugly truth.

Our willingness to unlock the door marked –

Keep Out!

leads us down our path of discovering the answers to many thoughts and feelings that never were addressed.

Deep down within the silent thoughts of my heart, I had suspected that somewhere in the early years of childhood, Phil had been subjected to either physical or sexual abuse. These unspoken suspicions arose from certain behaviors I saw and lived out in our marriage. I, like so many others, was never willing to take the risk of sharing the innermost secret thoughts of my heart's speculations concerning abuse. I often wondered why or how could someone so loving and caring be so mad or angry with me and the world around him.

I recall one day out of the blue Phil asked me if I had ever been abused sexually. My answer was no. Since he brought up the subject, I took the opportunity of asking, "Phil, have you ever been abused?"

Wrong question to ask. I remember Phil getting defensive and mad, so I told myself to never ask that question again.

Diving deeper into the private matters of my heart, I knew deep down that we had so many unresolved issues. I hoped one day I would have answers to all of my questions. What I had come to realize was in saying yes to living my life with Phil, honoring the commitment of our marriage vows until death do us part, that I was allowing myself to enter into the pain, which brought on a lot of suffering that my soulmate had lived with since his early childhood –

From being bullied to becoming a bully

From being abused to becoming the abuser

Drugs, sex, and alcohol became the "go to" antidotes to cover up the hidden shame and pain, which resulted in the stronghold of addictions.

I was totally aware of the addictive personality of my husband. Sometimes I went along with it just to keep peace. My perspective on discovering the ugly truth, as I recall, goes something like this:

I left the country to travel overseas to visit our daughter in Honduras in November of 2008 for three weeks. Upon returning home, I had discovered the stronghold of sexual addiction (some refer to it as pornography) had reared its ugly self once again. This discovery had left my spirit bound in grief, sadness, and a state of inner mourning for my husband. I knew it had nothing to do with me or against who I was to Phil as a wife. I just wanted the solution to fix it. I never shared or exposed the ugly truth to anyone. I knew that God is always at work in our lives. All I could do was pray that God would open the door of communication and allow me to confront Phil on this matter of sexual addiction.

Early spring of 2009, Phil was invited to preach a revival at First Baptist of Bowling Green, Florida, where he would partner with the First Impression, a contemporary Christian music group. It was at the end of the service one night when Phil challenged the people to turn to each other and simply ask, "Is everything okay with you?"

His younger brother, Danny, turned to me to ask. While I responded yes, I stood there wanting to scream out, *No, it is not okay! And Danny, you are not the one I need to talk to.*

As this inner battle was raging inside of me, I prayed, *Lord, will we ever be able to speak the ugly truth out loud? I hope one day we can have the freedom to tell it like it is.* It was at that moment that Phil had turned the invitation over to the pastor and walked off the stage to be by my side. Phil turned to me and asked, "Is everything okay with you?"

I looked at him and said yes. It was at that moment I realized God had just opened the door for me to walk through. I felt safe, so I then said, "No, actually it is not. But now is not the time or place to talk it out. Let's talk when we get back to the house."

The revival service ended. Lights were turned off. Then the doors were shut and locked. Everyone left to head back home. Now was the time to confront the ugly truth one-on-one. I was not sure how it would turn out, but I knew I could no longer stay silent. I had already given voice to an issue that needed to be heard. I will say I did feel an inner strength and courage to finally not be silent any longer.

Phil and I met in the room where we were staying. As Phil lay propped up against the pillows, I said, "Phil, I am not here to accuse you of anything or condemn you. After returning home from Honduras, I discovered the porn sites on the computer."

Phil graciously acknowledged that I was correct. He said he had already shared about giving into the temptation with his accountability partner. My respect for Phil had just risen to a higher level. We discussed the situation. I looked at Phil and dug deeper into the "why" question that I felt needed to be addressed. I said something like this, "I know that somewhere in your childhood, a door had to be opened up to allow the Enemy to come in."

What happened next, I never imagined would have taken place. At that moment Phil broke down and shared for the first time that he had been sexually abused by an older man when he was just a young boy.

My heart broke for my husband. I remember saying, "If

I could take this from you, I would." I felt so helpless at that moment and could only hold onto Phil as we lay there and cried.

Never in a million years would I have thought that this would be the last brick knocked down – the last brick that kept us bound for so many years. Healing started that night in our marriage. I knew that we would be able to completely share our story with the world. I felt as if I fell in love all over again. Now, allow me to shed some more light on this ugly truth.

I'm a dreamer. I cannot begin to express how I was able to connect the dots of this longstanding dream. On several occasions, I had a recurring dream. This dream dealt with a little boy who was crying out because of the pain of sexual abuse. Always after waking up, I would heartily pray for this boy somewhere in the world that has been abused or was being abused. I hadn't known that I had been praying for my husband, lover, and best friend.

You see, only when we refuse to stay silent and begin to address the ugly truth can we expect the miracle of healing and restoration to happen. When we share our ugly truth, the grief and pain of our past, we can experience a walk in freedom from bondage of sin and sorrow.

And you shall know the truth,
and the truth shall make you free. (John 8:32)

Reflect with me on the question: When will I ever be able to share how it really is?

Twenty-eight years of longsuffering had unfolded, which allowed truth to set Phil free from the bondage of addictions. You see, in sharing our ugly truth, we have chosen not to remain silent, hiding, or covering up who we really are in Christ Jesus. I urge you, like we did, to:

- Confess up and speak up.

- Dare to live your life out loud.

- Continue on; the best is yet to come!

After all, it is the ugly truth that hurts, not truth.

I am so thankful I did not quit. Today, Team Wade is enjoying the freedom of loving one another more deeply as we continue to share the ugly truth.

Deconstruction Begins – Back to Phil's Perspective

Well, there you have it, straight from the one bold and brave enough to stay in the game and keep fighting!

Life goes on, as the opportunities to pour life into our families speed by quickly. Time is among the most precious commodities we have in life. Once it is gone, it is gone forever. We can certainly rebuild what has been torn down, but the scars remain a part of our lives, and the time we could have spent more productively are lost. Sad, right?

Allowing Satan to drag us away from God with voices of shame, regret, embarrassment, and the mourning of lost time are tactics in Satan's plan to make us ineffective for the kingdom while we wallow around in our past. Someone once said that our past is in our heads, while our future is in God's hands.

My problem with this statement was that I had spent a lifetime as the captain of my ship, and up to this point, nothing but my cries of Mayday had been heard. Suddenly, having someone else – God – in charge of my life sounded good, especially after recalling the conversation when my wife told my doctor, "His kids are afraid of him, and if you do not fix him, I am leaving him."

That is Satan's plan: to drag us far away from the reality of who we really are, far away from loving unselfishly, and far away from God. We are born with a sinful nature, with Satan pulling us one way while the Holy Spirit draws us to God by speaking our worth in Christ into our spirit.

Regardless of what lies you may have bought into, what hellish consequences you have imposed on yourself, or what uncontrollable circumstances have altered your course, these things need not define you. The deconstruction of this false identity starts with the question, Why?

- Why am I here?

- How did I get here?

- What must I change?

- How can I experience freedom?

The last question is the most important one. Life gets tougher before it gets better. Take the step; deconstruction first, then reconstruction through spiritual renewal, a personal CPR. Great, healthy vital signs are just around the corner.

CHAPTER 3

THE VITALITY OF FORGIVING SELF AND OTHERS

S ome say people struggle more with one sin than any other sin.

- This sin keeps us from maximizing our potential as believers.

- This sin locks us in a cage from which we have already been set free.

- This sin often holds us in bondage to someone else's wrongdoing.

- This sin is the lack of forgiveness or an unwillingness to forgive. I am not just talking about withholding forgiveness from others. I am also talking about not forgiving ourselves.

Once the ugly truth was brought to light, I had to come to terms with it and its effect on myself and my family. I would love to say that a revelation of the effects of my falsely constructed identity and a plan of action to heal came in the next day's mail, but that would be a huge lie. The truth is, I am still learning of the effects to this day, as God continues to reveal all that I need to know moment by moment.

In order to walk in the forgiveness of self and others, we must first understand the love that God has for us. He demonstrated His love by His great desire to forgive us. God paid the price with His beloved Son in order to purchase our lives, which are slaves to sin.

During one of the most difficult seasons of my life, my wife confronted me with the question that caused me to come face to face with a desire to stop living a lie. I was tired of living as a stranger to myself, in fear of the rejection of others, God, and my family. As a rebellious teenager, I was told that I would never amount to anything. This led me to a performance-based life of workaholism to prove wrong those who breathed that curse on me. Living your life for others' approval only allows them to write your story instead of allowing God to take the lead.

My true identity had been buried beneath my mistakes, others' wrong doings, insecurities, and the lies of Satan. Bitterness had positioned me to become a destructive force in the lives of family and friends. The tremendous weight of the guilt I shouldered is what I believe to be the reason I have struggled with forgiving myself.

An important question to ask is what happens when we do not forgive? When the wound of unforgiveness is left open, infection sets in and blocks the healing. Bitterness then leads to resentment, which leads to anger, then deepens to malice, evolves into hatred, and ultimately winds up at the door of vengeance – the desire to hurt those who have hurt you.

Forgiveness

I could list many reasons to forgive ourselves and others, but I am going to focus on two:

(1) Forgiveness is without a doubt the greatest gift ever given to us. It is called a gift because we carry a debt of sin that we are unable to pay apart from the gift of the shed blood of Jesus. Our sin, guilt, shame, bitterness, and hatred have been forgiven, cancelled, paid in full. We have been set free from the prison that is sin's debt.

> *In Him we have redemption through His blood, the forgiveness of sins, according to the riches of His grace.* (Ephesians 1:7)

> *If we confess our sins, He is faithful and just to forgive us our sins and to cleanse us from all unrighteousness.* (1 John 1:9)

(2) When we have personally received and embraced God's forgiveness for our broken condition, we are able to forgive others who have hurt and wronged us.

I recognize this is "easy preaching and hard living." Plus, if I am going to stay transparent, I must admit I still struggle with holding grudges at times. And yes, that is lack of forgiveness with a different label. So, what does God say about this?

> *And forgive us our debts, as we forgive our debtors. And do not lead us into temptation but deliver us from the evil one. For Yours is the kingdom and the power and the glory forever. Amen. For if you forgive men their trespasses, your heavenly Father will also forgive you. But if you do not forgive men their trespasses, neither will your Father forgive your trespasses.* (Matthew 6:12-15)

The word *forgive* in the first verse means "to bear the burden." It always costs to forgive. The one doing the forgiving always pays.

It cost God His Son. If you owe someone one thousand dollars and they forgive your debt, it costs them a thousand dollars.

The progression of forgiveness, however, does not stop there. For example, God forgives Phil, and then tells Phil to go and forgive all who have hurt him. Consider the implications of last verse: *But if you do not forgive men their trespasses, neither will your Father forgive your trespasses.* According to that text, if we are unwilling to forgive others, then God turns us over to the painful consequences of our own lack of forgiveness.

Because the depth of the hurt in which you may live, you may have adopted the I-refuse-to-ever-forgive-them mentality. If that is you, please answer this question:

Are you tormented by your past sin, guilt, and shame, even though you profess Jesus as your Savior?

If your answer is yes, then it could be due to an unwillingness to forgive others while holding tight to the desire to serve your own justice on those who have offended you. It is vitally important to remember Jesus forgave you.

Justice belongs to God. Until we forgive, our jail time continues. Forgiveness is not about forgetting. We forgive others because God forgave us, and we refuse to remind those we have forgiven of their past offense. Allow me to breathe this hard truth into you. If you choose to receive and embrace this truth, it will be a healing balm to your open wound.

Bitterness

While in my second year of serving as lead pastor to a beautiful body of believers in Ocala, Florida, I was confronted about dealing with bitterness in a huge way. I received a phone call from a Christian businessman in Ocala who was attending my church. I knew him but did not have a close relationship with him at that point. We made plans for lunch.

I arrived early at the restaurant. A few minutes later, this gentleman, Greg Litton, and another one of my church members entered. What I thought would be a time of getting to know Greg and learning about his family, his relationship with Jesus, and his love for his work wound up being quite different. We discussed all the above topics, but his questions set me back and set my life on a new course.

Let me take you on this confessional journey:

Question Number One:
"Phil, is there a financial debt that you have been stuck with that has caused you to be bitter?"

Before I could answer, my mind ran wild as I thought, *First of all, who do you think you are, asking me this; and secondly, how did you know?*

Of course, I shared none of my thoughts, but simply answered yes.

Question Number Two:
"Phil, how can you stand before your people as their under-shepherd and speak of forgiveness when you yourself have lack of forgiveness and bitterness in your heart?"

"Greg," I responded, "that is a great question."

It is vitally important for you to understand that at this point, I wanted to punch him.

Question Number Three:
"Phil, what will you do about this lack of forgiveness and bitterness?"

"I guess a trip to see this individual is the only way I know to handle it the right way," I replied. Greg told me to let him know how it went after I met with this individual.

It was Thanksgiving. I had planned a round of golf with this fellow with whom I had become so bitter. Little did I know that this golf outing would be the theater in which God would do His healing work in both of our lives. Though I tried to make myself bring up the topic of my hurt and bitterness, only after the round of golf was over was the stage set.

I asked this man not to respond until I was finished. I took a deep breath before sharing my hurt, misunderstanding, and feelings of betrayal. I poured out my heart for forty-five minutes. Many tears were shed before I finished. I asked him not to try to explain away the situation, but to please forgive me for being bitter and holding a grudge.

"Phil, I am so sorry," he said with tears flowing down his face. "I didn't know what else to do. Certainly, I forgive you, but will you, please, forgive me?"

Of course, I did. What seemed to be prison doors were opened! The shackles fell off, and what had been a beautiful, strong relationship that had gone bad was now restored.

The financial debt I had to assume was eighty-thousand dollars with a one-thousand-dollar-a-month payment that had all but ruined my family. At this point in the story, I still owed forty thousand dollars. So, what did forgiving this debt cost me? Forty thousand dollars!

Freedom

Back home in Ocala, Florida, weeks later, the phone rang. Guess who it was? Yep, "Mr. Prophet" himself, Greg Litton.

"Phil, how was your trip?"

"Greg, God performed a miracle!"

"Let us do lunch. I want to hear about it."

We met days later for barbeque and great fellowship at Greg's place of business. After sharing the story of how God had so beautifully worked in this reconciliation, Greg asked me to push my pause button long enough for him to speak.

"Phil, God has called each of us to forgive others and reconcile our differences. That is exactly what you have done. But God has also called me to play a role in this story. Phil, how much of the debt do you still owe?"

"Forty thousand dollars," I replied.

"Well, God called you to forgive, and He has called me to assume the remainder of your debt. Phil, Nathaniel and I also know your truck is on its last leg. God has laid on Nathaniel's heart to give you his truck."

What? I could not believe my ears. Was I in a dream?

Greg continued, "That is right, the remainder of the debt you assumed and a 2007 Dodge Ram 1500 Hemi 4-door, candy apple red and chrome truck is yours."

This story must sound as crazy to you as it did for me when he offered these gifts. However, to know Greg the way I do now is to know his heart of obedience and his generous spirit.

After picking myself up off the floor, I said, "Don't be joking around with me. This would be too cruel a prank. Then, potentially, I would struggle with forgiving you. All joking aside, do these gifts come with strings attached? Because God may have me give the truck away one day." (That is a story for another time.)

Praise

After his affirming answer, "No strings attached," we all celebrated the goodness of God with many tears and much laughter. To tell you the truth, for the rest of the day I was walking on cloud nine.

- God promises provision. Our job is to walk in obedience.

- We are to be rivers, not reservoirs.

- God gives forgiveness, and we are to offer the same to others.

That was the day I began to live out Isaiah 61:1-3 in living color:

> *The Spirit of the Lord GOD is upon Me, Because the LORD has anointed Me to preach good tidings to the poor; He has sent Me to heal the brokenhearted, To proclaim liberty to the captives, And the opening of the prison to those who are bound; To proclaim the acceptable year of the LORD, And the day of vengeance of our God; To comfort all who mourn, To console those who mourn in Zion, To give them beauty for ashes, The oil of joy for mourning, The garment of praise for the spirit of heaviness; That they may be called trees of righteousness, The planting of the LORD, that He may be glorified.*

That day I put on *the garment of praise* and threw away *the spirit of heaviness* that the lack of forgiveness had weighed me down with for decades. That day I stopped focusing on my past, my problems, my pain, and my guilt, and I began focusing on the solution.

We have not been called to submit to our problems or fix our problems or those of others. We have been called to submit to the only, sure-fire prescription for our brokenness and this broken world. The healing solution is none other than the Son of the Living God, Jesus Christ.

Follow His prescription:

- Accept His forgiveness.

- Leave the torment.

- Put on the *garment of praise*.

CHAPTER 4

DISCOVERING THE MISSION

I finally had to acknowledge that I was tired of simply existing. I was sick and tired of being sick and tired. I had no life, passion, energy, excitement, or purpose. I was living behind the wall of the false identity I had constructed to gain the approval of others. I was living a lie; I had convinced myself I was someone who I was not and, furthermore, someone whom I hated.

My wife was the one who helped me discover that living this lie was harming my family and me personally. That was when I realized I needed personal revival, a spiritual CPR. I had to make a decision to do things differently and discover a new way to do life. I needed to see myself, my family, and even my offenders through the eyes of God. This realization allowed me to begin the process of forgiving myself, forgiving others, and asking for the forgiveness of others.

This led me to some of the most life-altering discoveries imaginable – my purpose in life, the way God wired me, why I like the things I like and dislike the things I dislike, and those things that light my fire, crank my tractor, and awaken me each morning with excitement and enthusiasm to start my day.

Searching

On what seemed to be a typical Sunday morning at Calvary Baptist Church in St. Augustine, Florida, the worship music ended, and my pastor, Dr. Mark Conrad – one of the greatest men of integrity I have ever met as well as one of my dearest friends – stood to preach from the book of Philippians. No reflection on Dr. Conrad's teaching or his ability to communicate, but I heard nothing that he preached. The seemingly typical turned nontypical in a hurry. My mind and heart went to a place that I could not explain. While I was not sobbing out loud, tears streamed down my face for the next forty minutes.

At some point during this time, Keli leaned over and asked, "What is wrong?"

"I don't know," was the only honest answer I could give.

As we drove home to our apartment on Anastasia Island after the service, Keli broke the silence and asked me if I wanted to hear what she believed was my inner struggle. I said yes, because I knew I was about to hear it anyway. Her words, though calming, resonated within my spirit and led me to discover the greatest journey of my spiritual life, one that I am still walking today.

"Phil," she said, "what you are currently struggling with, and have been for some time, is fear – the fear of living your dream, the fear of saying yes and surrendering to the call God has placed on your life. You know God has called you to preach. Although serving other pastors is a noble calling, it is time for you to go live your dream."

At this moment my heart beat as it had never beaten before. With excitement, I told Keli that if God was truly calling me to be a lead pastor of a church, He would have to make that happen, because I refused to try to manipulate God's agenda for my life. Now, I must admit that trying to manipulate and fast forward God's plans for my life was, and can still be, an issue for this ole boy, but it was not in this circumstance. Why? The fear of unworthiness.

This fear manifested itself when I refused to send resumes unless a church first called me to ask for one. Well, God knew what I was doing and why. In only a matter of three to four weeks, we received three phone calls from three different churches in three different states. Okay, now God had my attention.

After weeks of many emails, phone conversations, several phone interviews, and a lot of praying, we took a weekend to go spend time with one of the churches in Georgia. We discovered that our DNAs were completely different, and this marriage between pastor and church was not in God's plan. One down, and two to go. The anticipation of how God was going to position us to do what we believed He had called us to do was exciting, but exhausting.

New Dreams

Several weeks later, Keli and I visited Trinity Baptist Church in Ocala, Florida. Their pulpit search committee was extremely inviting, for the most part. The search team started by sharing their vision of what they were looking for in a pastor. After a little Q&A to get my mind wrapped around what was taking place among their church body, I shared that the most important thing for Keli and me was to be in the center of God's will regardless of where that took us geographically. We spent a lot of time laying out our vision for what we believed God would have us do, if He called us to under-shepherd this church. We shared candidly with the committee that we had declined one church, but both Trinity and a church in Tennessee were still on God's drawing board. One of the leaders then shared that they would continue to pray and seek God's will for the future of Trinity Baptist Church. We prayed and hugged necks after they told us they would be in touch with us soon.

Keli and I enjoyed the forty-five-minute ride back to our apartment in St. Augustine, Florida. This ride home was fun. It was different as it was filled with the anticipation of God's birthing what we had dreamed of for years, but what I had possibly delayed by walking in fear. We prayed together. We laughed together. We cried together. We celebrated the fact that our hearts were beginning to beat together in a whole new way.

The next morning I knew, without a doubt, that God had spoken to me – and told me that I should call the church in Tennessee to request they remove my name from their list of candidates because God had called us in a different direction. Validated by my wife, I felt with certainty God was calling us to Ocala, Florida, even though the pastor search committee had not confirmed it themselves.

Moving Forward

A few weeks later a member of the search committee called and asked if we could do lunch. Because he needed to be in Jacksonville, Florida, we were able to meet that week. During our lunch meeting that Friday, the gentleman shared that the committee felt a great need to do their due diligence by continuing to evaluate four or five other pastoral candidates. I assured him that I felt that was best for everyone involved and encouraged them to move forward with their plan. The problem, he said, was that they knew we had another church considering us and did not want that opportunity to slip through our hands. So, I told him that several days earlier I had contacted the church in Tennessee and told them to remove my name from the list.

"Why did you do that?" he asked.

I responded that Keli and I were confident that God was

calling us to Ocala. We simply were waiting on Him to tell the search committee of the news that we would be their next pastor. We laughed, high-fived, ate some good Sonny's barbecue, and said our goodbyes. We left each other knowing, without ever saying so, that soon we would talk.

The Call

A couple of weeks later, I received a phone call asking that we come to Ocala to meet with the people of the church and preach in view of a call. It happened just as God said it would happen. About sixty days later, we began living the dream that God had called us to live as the lead pastor of Trinity Baptist Church. The mission had been discovered. My calling was to undershepherd the people of God – to teach them to do the work of the ministry and love them as God had called us to love them.

Motivational Gifts

One of the things I learned through this is the difference between the discovery of your mission and the knowledge of how to accomplish that mission with great effectiveness. In this new role I had to learn the art of time management, the art of becoming intentional, and the art of essentialism versus non-essentialism. I had to dare to say no to the good, which has always been difficult for me, so that we could accomplish the great. I had to learn five things about serving:

- God is not looking for talented people.
- God is looking for people who make themselves available.
- In and of ourselves we do not have what it takes.

- God will equip whomever He calls to do whatever he calls them to do.
- With the power of the Holy Spirit of God and His gifting, all things are possible.

If this were not the case, I would not be doing what God has called me to do today. Why? Because in and of myself, I do not have what it takes. As I sought to serve God's people with maximum effectiveness, I had to discover my gifts and be clear about them.

Only by the calling, gifting, and empowering of God through His Holy Spirit could I dare take on this responsibility.

Apostle Paul addresses these motivational gifts in Romans 12:3-8:

> For I say, through the grace given to me, to everyone who is among you, not to think of himself more highly than he ought to think, but to think soberly, as God has dealt to each one a measure of faith. For as we have many members in one body, but all the members do not have the same function, so we, being many, are one body in Christ, and individually members of one another. Having then gifts differing according to the grace that is given to us, let us use them: if prophecy, let us prophesy in proportion to our faith; or ministry, let us use it in our ministering; he who teaches, in teaching; he who exhorts, in exhortation; he who gives, with liberality; he who leads, with diligence; he who shows mercy, with cheerfulness.

Paul makes clear in these verses that believers have gifts that are given according to the grace of God. Then he simply describes the seven gifts.

Peter calls us to minister these gifts to one another as good stewards of God's grace, operate in these gifts according to the ability that God gives, and in all things, make sure God gets the glory:

> As each one has received a gift, minister it to one
> another, as good stewards of the manifold grace of
> God. If anyone speaks, let him speak as the oracles
> of God. If anyone ministers, let him do it as with
> the ability which God supplies, that in all things
> God may be glorified through Jesus Christ, to whom
> belong the glory and the dominion forever and ever.
> Amen. (1 Peter 4:10-11)

The Purpose

When we identify our gifts and recognize that they are not for our benefit but for the benefit of others and glory of God, then we can thrive. Going to church is not about what we can get, though in most instances I have been blessed while worshipping with other believers. Going to church is about doing life with our fellow believers to determine what we can give. It is loving and serving God by serving people with our gifts. That is my calling, my mission, and my purpose. Likewise, it is your calling, mission, and purpose. We do not do it out of selfish motivation; we do it all for the glory of God!

I was blessed when I realized that my calling was not just to be a disciple, but that I was to use my gifts and calling to be a disciple-maker. I cannot explain in human terms the joy that comes when we take our focus off our own fleshly desires and meet the needs of those around us through our giftedness and the love of Christ.

I know what I am about to say may sound crazy to some, but –

- In serving myself, I never seem to find satisfaction.

- By serving others, I cannot contain the joy it brings.

A true indicator of our spiritual growth is our obedient walk in what we know God has called us to do. We must therefore discover how He has gifted us to do it.

What are these motivational gifts about? They are the expression of God's grace working in each believer. Yes, these gifts are given to each believer to carry out the work of the ministry that God calls us to do. These gifts do not come through the call of our moms, dads, or grandparents. These gifts are distributed by God through His sovereignty and grace.

Could it be that many people are miserable in their lives because they are operating outside of their giftedness? That is not God's intention for us.

- Salvation Past: Most believers understand salvation past – that is, as believers, we are saved by the shed blood of Jesus.

- Salvation Future: We also get salvation future – that is, as believers, we will spend eternity in heaven.

- Salvation Present: We often struggle with this because we do not operate in salvation present. We swim in the despair of broken marriages, rebellious kids, sexual perversions, and materialism, even though Jesus died to free us from the bondage of present sin, so we can operate in our giftedness for the benefit of others and glory of God.

The Lesson

Every Christian has at least one gift given to us by God, and every Christian views other people, circumstances, books he reads, and songs he sings – everything – through the lens of his motivational gifts. Seven people see the same thing seven different ways.

I will never forget how I was so quick to voice my frustration early in our marriage when things did not go my way or when Keli did not do things the way I thought they should be done. Then one day Keli said, "Phil, when will you see that our differences should not frustrate us? Rather, they should excite us, because it is our differences that make us complete."

That one was a punch in the gut! I could not deny its truth. Once again, my vision became a little clearer. It might help you to understand that the only things my wife and I have in common are our faith, children, and grandchildren. It is true that opposites attract. We are proof of that. It is also true that if we refused to see others through the eyes of God and appreciate how He has created us all to be unique, we would be headed down a dead-end street in attack mode when we are not getting our way.

The following seven gifts are called motivational because they are the motivating forces of our lives. For me, I have discovered that my strongest gift is the gift of exhortation. I love encouraging people, not because I am paid to do it, but because it is who God made me. When I am walking in the Spirit, I am an encourager. But when walking in the flesh, I can be as hateful as any human being on this planet.

We either use our gifts appropriately to serve others and to honor God, or we misuse them and people get hurt. Sometimes we do not use them at all and find ourselves simply existing, feeling like life has no meaning or purpose. Allow me to describe each of the seven gifts. My hope is that you might find yourself in one of them and begin your journey of walking in God's gift to you for the good of others and for His glory.

The Prophet

The biblical prophet is not only one who foresees the plans of God, but they also forthtell the mind and the heart of God. They proclaim the truth that already has been spoken and bring sin to light. I believe this gift is my wife's number-one motivational gift. With her it is black and white, period. If we do not understand this about the person with the gift of prophecy, conflict will result, and someone's going to get offended. A misuse of this gift could be insensitivity and lack of mercy, so we must use them as we are empowered by the Holy Spirit of God.

The Servant

Those with the gift of service love every opportunity they get to serve and meet the needs of others. This brings them energy and purpose daily. To understand the person with the gift of serving is also to know that they are willing to sign up for just about anything. Because they are people pleasers, they often forget to ask the Lord if this service opportunity is what He would have them do. As a pastor, I have learned that servant-gifted people, if abused and hurt, can become vicious in their anger. Servant-gifted people can also get trapped in "doing" to the point of bringing physical harm to themselves and causing dissension in the home.

The Teacher

These are the individuals who love research, information, and details. They love to clarify truth regardless of its source. They will validate information given to them most often before they share it. "Tell me more. Let's go deeper" is their mantra. The misuse of this gift can often be valuing their knowledge more than the people they are teaching. Many times, they can frustrate the listener with far too many details and way too little practical application. This group is intense because they love sharing what they have discovered through their studies and research.

Exhortation

I believe with every fiber of my being this is my number-one gift. This group lives with the inward drive to encourage others to live a winning life. When walking in the Spirit of God, they are extremely positive, outgoing people. Our weakness can often be putting off the hard truth in fear of losing the relationship. In doing this we bring false hope. We must not ever delay the hard truth that God calls us to deliver, regardless of the consequences. Many times, the right words, at the right time, and in the right place bring about great healing, though it may take time.

Giving

This is the group that loves to give of their time, their talent, their treasure, and their energy. They love doing whatever is necessary in the area of giving to move the church and the gospel forward. These individuals are not necessarily people with a lot of money. They are simply people who maximize their time, talent, and treasure in the area of giving in order to get results.

The Leader

The leader – the administrator, organizer, facilitator, and the one who loves to direct traffic – is the one who loves to plan and get the job done. This is the group of people who will run over people in order to complete the project if they are not careful, when the project was for those very people. Leaders must avoid, at all costs, the temptation to operate in all seven gifts, because in doing so, they can sideline many other gifted people who desire to be a part of God's big-picture plan.

Mercy

When it comes to the gift of mercy, I can tell you beyond a shadow of a doubt that there has never been anyone in my eyes who rises above my mother in showcasing this gift with great humility. This lady, a beautiful example of this group of people, really knows how to care for others. They are always thinking with their hearts and always thinking about others before themselves. The misuse of this gift is that the mercy gifted person can often short circuit God's plan in the lives of people in the area of correction. They cannot stand to see people hurt and live to take away the pain of others at whatever cost.

The seven different motivational gifts are for believers who form the one body of Christ that has different parts with different passions and functions in the body.[2]

- The teacher is the body's mind.

- The prophet is the body's eyes.

- The exhorter is the body's mouth.

- The leader is the body's shoulders (carrying the burden of getting it done)

---

2   Reference to 1 Corinthians 12:12-31.

- Mercy is the body's heart.
- The giver is the body's arms.
- The server is the body's hands.

One of the ways to discern your motivational gift is to ask, why do you want to serve other people?

The Discovery

Another way to identify your motivational gifts is to examine your irritations. For me, it irritates me to hear preachers who do not encourage others. Why? It is the way I view things as I am an encourager.

When believers embrace the fact that we are all ministers of the gospel and understand that we have been created, saved, called, authorized, and ultimately rewarded for our ministry, it is then that we will begin to move forward as warriors, royal priests, and people of courage.

I am sure there are many reasons people are not operating in their motivational gift. Maybe they have never been taught about these gifts. Perhaps, the teaching on these gifts was confusing. You may be one of these individuals who either does not know what your gift is or how to operate in it.

- First, let me encourage you to discover your gift.

- Second, through prayer and maybe the help of a friend, a pastor, or a leader, begin to write a purpose statement for yourself.

- Third, find a life verse that supports the gifting and the purpose that God has called you to live out.

- Last, I would encourage you to find what I call a life word.

For example, here is what it looks like for me: (1) My number-one gift is the gift of exhortation. My number-two gift is leadership; (2) My purpose statement is to develop godly leaders and encourage them to live life beyond themselves; (3) My life verse is Matthew 6:33: *Seek first the kingdom of God and His righteousness and all these things shall be added unto you*; and (4) My life word is intentional.

Using this framework: Every day when my feet hit the floor, I intentionally seek first the kingdom of God and his righteousness; I trust Him with everything else while I go about my day, developing godly leaders and encouraging them to live life beyond themselves.

I pray you can see how discovering my mission has changed my life. With 100% certainty I know that if you discover yours, it will change your life too. The question is, Will you dare to discover your mission? Will you dare to face your fears head on? As author John Ortberg writes, "If you want to walk on water, you have to get out of the boat."

Your mission is to discover your story so that you may live your legacy. If our hearts are ever to beat afresh and anew, and if we are ever to experience the thrill of walking on water, it is vital that we experience spiritual CPR.

I double-dog dare you to relinquish control of your life and permit God to have His way with you.

CHAPTER 5

A HEART FOR THE CASTAWAY

Have you ever walked past a homeless person and wondered how they got where they are? Maybe you have even come eye to eye with the street beggar at a red light and caught yourself turning your head in order to ignore him. Have you ever visited a prison and realized the only difference between a prisoner and many of us is that they got caught and we did not? Have you ever heard of someone's suicide and made a statement like, "I would have never done something so selfish." Maybe you have traveled abroad and walked among the filth and the stench of poverty. Did it cause you to pause and ponder, "Why them and not me?" Did it snap you into the reality that such a fate is still in the realm of possibility for you? For me, every one of these questions scream the answer yes! I have said it, thought it, and done it.

I have walked past a homeless person, wondered why they were homeless but totally ignored them. I have preached in many a prison and wondered how I escaped the striped suit. I have ignored the beggar at the red light. I have criticized those who committed suicide. I have even walked on five of the seven continents and seen poverty at its worst. And still I wonder today, why them and not me? Even in writing this chapter, I hate using the words *they* and *them*. I feel as though I am putting them in a category of something less than human.

That is not my heart at all, but when busyness and self-centeredness become our lifestyle, it becomes easy to turn our backs on people and judge what is not the norm for us. Sometimes we may even view ourselves as loftier than we are and forget about those of whom Jesus wished to heal and to save.

Jesus often spoke of the broken, the prodigal, the outcast, and less fortunate. They are the ones for whom He came to die. The Bible tells us that Jesus came to seek and to save that which was lost (Luke 19:10). If that is the truth, and it is, then that puts us all in the same category of the broken, the prodigal, the outcast, and the less fortunate. We all stand on even ground when it comes to our need to be rescued.

Perspective of Faith

Let's look at the outcast from two viewpoints: spiritual and social perspectives.

(1) Spiritual Perspective of the Outcast

Based on the Word of God, apart from Jesus we are all outcasts:

- *For all have sinned and fall short of the glory of God* (Romans 3:23). Sin is what prevents us from having a personal, intimate relationship with God.

- *For the wages of sin is death, but the gift of God is eternal life in Christ Jesus our Lord* (Romans 6:23). Through Jesus, and Him alone, we can be delivered from spiritual death, separation from God, and receive eternal life.

- *For God so loved the world that He gave His only begotten Son, that whoever believes in Him should not perish but have everlasting life* (John 3:16). Remember, God never intended for anyone to live outside of fellowship with Him.

- *For the Son of Man has come to seek and to save that which was lost* (Luke 19:10). The lost are all of us prior to accepting the redemption gift of God's only Son, Jesus.

- *For whoever calls on the name of the LORD shall be saved* (Romans 10:13). Calling out to God in confession of our sin, repenting of our sin, declaring our need for His forgiveness, and then placing our faith in His shed blood are the steps in our journey from being a spiritual outcast to becoming a child of the living God.

But before we move to our second perspective on the outcast, please allow me to use my gift of encouragement. If we are ever to receive a renewing of the heart – spiritual CPR – then we must take the truths I just shared seriously and place our faith in the Son of God, Jesus Christ.

Have you done this? If not, please know that it is the longing of God's heart to call you His own. Please pause right now and pray with me.

Father God,

In the name of Jesus, I confess to you that I am a person of sin. I confess that apart from the shed blood of Your Son, Jesus, I am doomed an outcast, to be separated from You for eternity. Please forgive me of my sin. I choose this day to place my faith in the work of Jesus and receive the free gift of salvation which only comes through Him. I thank you today for adopting me, a former outcast, into the family of God.

In Jesus's name, Amen.

I pray that if you trusted Christ as your Savior today, you will tell somebody. Tell your pastor, if you have one. Tell a believing friend or a co-worker. Seek out the right spiritual guidance as to the next step in your journey. Finding a Christian community will be essential to growing and maintaining a spiritually healthy heart.

Allow me to say, "Congratulations!" I cannot even begin to tell you how excited I am for you, not to mention that the angels in heaven are rejoicing over you, the "new addition" to the family of God. Even the angels in heaven care that you are no longer an outcast. It is written in Luke 15:10: *Likewise, I say to you, there is joy in the presence of the angels of God over one sinner who repents.*

(2) Social Perspective of the Outcast

But what about the social outcast? As you have heard in my story in the previous chapters, that is exactly how I felt about myself. I believe that is why my heart beats for the outcast. In my journey, I have learned this important lesson.

There are fewer people who view others as outcasts than there are people who view themselves as outcasts.

Perspective of Fear

In the late fall/early winter, I was preparing for a trip to McLean, Texas, for a trophy deer hunt. I needed several large coolers to

Having dealt with many benevolent cases as a pastor, I must confess that his story really sounded sketchy. Pressing further, I asked George if he had a copy of the prescription. He told me he did and pulled the prescription out of his pocket. I told him that I would be stopping at the next drugstore to validate the truth of his story. If it checked out, I would purchase his medication.

Moments later, we exited off the interstate to find the closest drugstore. George and I walked inside, where I shared the story with a pharmacist. I asked if she could check to validate the prescription and George's story. About twenty minutes later, the pharmacist returned and told me that both his story and the prescription were valid. She had called the hospital in Tampa to verify George's story.

At this point my bitter, judgmental, self-consumed heart began to turn toward compassion for this man I had just met and who could possibly be an angel God had sent to get my mind off my negative, selfish spirit. I asked the pharmacist if I could purchase the prescription for George. She replied that I could, but it was very expensive. I told her I was not concerned with the cost but would like to make the purchase, which I did.

After leaving the drugstore, I asked George if I could stop and get him something to eat. He accepted my offer. As we drove up the interstate to find somewhere to eat, I talked to George about his relationship with the Lord. He assured me that in times past he had trusted the Lord. George said he talked to Jesus every day, and he used to read the Bible daily. However, because of sleeping under bridges that leaked water, his Bible had been destroyed. I reached into the backseat of my truck and handed George one of my own Bibles.

We soon found a place to eat and stopped for food. After eating we drove toward the truck stop where George wanted to be taken. I offered to take him to Jacksonville, but he declined my offer. I prayed for George and sent him on his way with a man hug.

I would love to tell you that my ten-minute ride home from George's drop-off point was a time of reflecting on the goodness of God. However, if I am to be honest, it was a time of kicking myself for my stinking attitude that almost caused me to miss of one of the greatest God-appointments of my life. George, a man I would never see again, forever changed my outlook on the down-trodden, those considered the outcasts of society.

The smell of this man lingered in my truck for days to come. After telling my wife the story of my encounter with George, she asked why I did not go clean the truck in order to get the smell out. I replied that for the first time in my life, the smell of the homeless caused me to think of Jesus. For days and weeks ahead, I could not help but share the story of my almost missed opportunity to entertain an angel.

Sadness Strikes

Weeks later, while visiting family in Rome, Georgia, I received a phone call from someone at my church who asked me to remind them of the man's name I had picked up and dropped off at the truck stop several weeks earlier. After sharing George's name with them, they said that in the middle of the night, George had been struck by a car and killed underneath the bridge next to the truck stop where I dropped him off. As if that was not bad enough news, the person who had hit George was a member my church.

When Keli and I returned to Ocala several days later, I had the opportunity to minister to the dear lady who had accidentally killed George. I shared with her that George had been hurting so badly for so long that he longed to be in heaven much more than he wanted to be here on earth. That knowledge comforted both of us. I was also comforted when I learned that the accident was not her fault. George, for whatever reason, had wandered out into the middle of the road in the pitch-black dark.

To say that I can make complete sense of how it all happened would be a major untruth. This I do know with certainty: God had a plan for bringing this man into my life and allowing me to see someone I considered an outcast through the eyes of Christ. Through this experience I learned that George had much more to offer me than I could ever offer him. The opportunity to minister to one of my own church family members brought much greater joy because we realized that the Lord had allowed me to give comfort to George in his final days. My heart hurt, yet my heart rejoiced to know that George would never face pain or rejection again, and he would spend eternity with the one who called him "His own." George: forever free. Me: forever changed. All because someone I considered an outcast needed a ride. Coincidence? I do not think so! God's getting my attention? Absolutely!

So why do you think we resist the people society considers social outcasts? Would it be because we do not understand them? I would say that is often the case. Could it be we are being judgmental? I would say that is true in some cases. But I would submit that a big reason is fear. We fear not knowing what to say, how to help, or being rejected.

Reality

Homeless people gather weekly at Reach Ministries in Rome, Georgia, for a meal and to hear the gospel shared as well as to get much-needed groceries, clothing, love, prayer, assistance with housing and bills, jobs, bicycles, and even vehicles. God gave a vision for this ministry to a remarkable lady named Merlene and her husband Leon, who was once considered an outcast.

Even being one of the boldest and most courageous couples I have ever met, Merlene and Leon face fear as they undertake and continue this vital ministry. I expect there are times when they wonder, *What if all the volunteers go away? What if the provision of food dries up? What if the need becomes greater than the supply?* Yet, this brave couple faithfully continue to serve God, as do the many volunteers who show up every week to serve tirelessly. Although society may see the weekly recipients of this ministry as outcasts, this is not how Merlene, Leon, and the many volunteers view these homeless individuals.

Now imagine for just a moment what it must be like to be on the receiving end of that line. What kind of fears do you think those people must face?

- The fear of being turned away yet another time.

- The fear that no one will look at me.

- The fear of what people think when they look at me.

- The fear that people are talking about me when I am not invited into a conversation.

- The fear that no one cares that I have a name, that I am labeled as an outcast, homeless, or a bum.

- The fear that no one wants to hear my story.

- The fear that no one really cares.

I know that some of you are thinking the same thing that I have thought before: *Why do they not just go and get a job?* And you know what? Yes, there are those who abuse the system. Many could simply go and get a job. However, please allow me to pause here and offer a few thoughts.

- Consider what God says about the poor. *There will always be poor people in the land* (Deuteronomy 15:11). In other words, regardless of how hard we try to fix the problem, there will always be someone somewhere who is experiencing poverty.

- Notice that God has a special place in His heart for what society would consider the outcast. *If one of your brethren becomes poor and falls into poverty among you, then you shall help him, like a stranger or sojourner, that he may live with you* (Leviticus 25:35). Live with me? Wow, now that one will bring on some fear and anxiety!

- Reflect on your reaction and actions for the poor. *Blessed is he who considers the poor; The Lord will deliver him in a time of trouble* (Psalm 41:1).

- Chew on this proverb: *He who oppresses the poor reproaches his Maker, but he who honors Him has mercy on the needy* (Proverbs 14:31).

- Ask God to reveal your heart as you consider this passage that has always found an "ouch" spot in my heart. *Then He also said to him who invited Him, "When you give a dinner or a supper, do not ask your friends, your brothers, your relatives, nor rich neighbors, lest they also invite you back, and you be repaid. But when you give a feast, invite the poor, the maimed, the lame, the blind. And you will be blessed, because they cannot repay you; for you shall be repaid at the resurrection of the just"* (Luke 14:12-14). You mean I am supposed to sacrifice for the outcast?

- Ponder your priorities as you reflect on these words of Jesus: *I needed clothes and you clothed Me, I was sick and you looked after me, I was in prison and you came to visit Me* (Matthew 25:36 NIV).

God's Heart

Being true, authentic followers of Christ means that our hearts for the outcast should beat the same as the Son of God's heart beats. As I have already confessed, my heart has not always been in the right place when it comes to this subject.

I had finished preaching at Reach Ministries' weekly feed when a man approached me and shared his need for different living arrangements. I asked him what was wrong with his current living conditions, and he explained that the man he shared the house with was involved in heavy use of heroine. This issue caused a tremendous struggle as he had only been clean of drugs himself for a short period of time, and heroin was his downfall. I assured him that it would certainly be in his best interest to remove himself from this situation or to help his roommate find another place. He told me that the house in which he was living was his roommate's house. When I learned that, I told him about a place I knew that was about twelve to fifteen miles away. I could tell by the look on the man's face that this would not work. He had no driver's license and needed to be within walking distance of work. I asked why he did not have a driver's license. His response forever changed my attitude of "just go get a job, people."

Like many of us, this man had made some poor choices in life that had cost him his family, his freedom, and his license. While serving time in prison, everything he had ever owned or held dear disappeared. This included driving privileges.

I asked when his driving privileges would be reinstated; He said they already had been, but his previous license and his birth certificate were nowhere to be found. Here is a question for all of us: Have you ever met someone whom you were certain had at one time been pretty sharp, but the power of drug addiction had robbed them of most of their ability to think or reason? Well, this was the person with whom I was dealing. I realized that he did not need a driver's license, even if we could retrieve all the proper information. However, his situation made me realize that many cases are not as easy as "just go get a job, people."

I understand that our lack of knowledge can cause us to view situations in an incorrect light. I also understand that while we have the power to choose, we do not have the power to choose the consequences. I get it that he made his choices and now is paying for his poor choices. Our responsibility is to extend the same grace that has been extended to us. We must remember that if not for the grace of God, so we may go. We cannot walk in fear of those who are different from us. We must remember God's Word and what He says to those who turn their backs on the outcast:

> *"I was a stranger and you did not take Me in, naked and you did not clothe Me, sick and in prison and you did not visit Me." Then they also will answer Him, saying, "Lord, when did we see You hungry or thirsty or a stranger or naked or sick or in prison, and did not minister to You?" Then He will answer them, saying, "Assuredly, I say to you, inasmuch as you did not do it to one of the least of these, you did not do it to Me." And these will go away into ever-lasting punishment, but the righteous into eternal life* (Matthew 25:43-46).

In my prodigal days, someone who did not know me well tried their best to help me. I will never forget saying these very words to them, "I am not a project; I am a person. Stop trying to fix me and get to know me."

Can I encourage you to join me in taking this view as we

see society's outcast the way Jesus sees them – as family? My prayer for each of us is that we will experience spiritual renewal when it comes to loving God and loving people. *Jesus said to him, "You shall love the LORD your God with all your heart, with all your soul, and with all your mind." This is the first and great commandment. And the second is like it: "You shall love your neighbor as yourself"* (Matthew 22:37-39).

CHAPTER 6

RELATIONSHIPS ARE THE KEY

Shortly after coming off the road from thirteen years of singing with First Impression, I sat with a senior pastor to interview for my first church staff position. Sometime during our conversation, I asked a question that I believe to be the most important question I have ever asked anyone concerning ministry. I received what I believe to be the greatest answer that I could have been given – an answer that would direct the course of my ministry for the rest of my life and be the game-changer above all game-changers.

"What is the key to ministry?" I asked.

"Relationships," the pastor responded without hesitation.

His one-word answer was so simple, yet so profound and right. Relationships are the key to our spiritual life, our marital life, friendships, and leadership. With no hesitation, I believe that they are unequivocally the key to our maximizing our earthly and heavenly existence. It begins with our relationship with Jesus and moves out from that central relationship to our relationships with others.

You have heard some of my story. It should be no surprise that the relationship between my father and me was often strained at best. As a young kid growing up under my father's roof, his method of teaching, discipline, and involvement in my life did not seem to reflect one of desiring a relationship with me. Now, as a father and grandfather myself with many more years under my belt, I realize that his method was not as off-base as my understanding of what he tried to accomplish as a father.

Prodigal

Allow me to introduce you to another young man, who reminds me of my prodigal self. He also struggled with the way his father did things. Time and circumstances allowed him to see the love of his father with a much clearer vision. I will let him tell you his story.

> According to the laws of my land, that being Jewish law, an older son should receive twice the inheritance as the younger sons, and fathers can give up their wealth during their lifetime if they so choose. It was perfectly legal for me, the younger son, to ask for my share of the estate and even to sell it if I chose to do so. I knew without a doubt that doing so was not the right thing to do. By doing that, I basically told my dad that I wished he no longer lived. Someone once said, "A man's worst difficulties begin when he is able to do as he pleases."
>
> I was headed for trouble when I valued things more than people, especially my family; the pleasures of this world more than my loyalty to my family and my duty as a son; the things of this world more than the blessings I had at home. I remember Jesus once warned two brothers who were arguing to take heed and beware of covetousness. It was so true because being a covetousness person, I was never satisfied no matter how much

I could get my hands on. A dissatisfied heart led to a life of disappointment. I was learning the hard way that I could never enjoy the things money could buy if I ignored the things money could not buy.

It seemed so innocent. I dreamed of enjoying my freedom as far away from my dad and my older brother as I could get. All I wanted was to do things my way. I rebelled and broke my family's heart. Life in the far country was not all I expected either. Food ran out, money ran out, my friends left, famine came to the land, and I was forced to do for a stranger that which I would not do for my own father: go to work.

Now as I look back, it becomes very clear what sin does in the lives of people when we reject the Father's will. Sin promised freedom, and I became a slave. It promised success, yet I failed miserably. It promised life, but spiritual death gloomed all around me. In the things of this world and freedom, I thought I would surely find myself only to realize that I was more lost than ever before.

To repent means to change your mind, which is exactly what I did as I cared for the pigs – not the dream job for a Jewish kid. But it was there that I found myself. For up to this point, I really had not been myself at all. My insanity clouded the image of God within me and unleashed a raging animal. At that point, I changed my mind about myself and about my salvation; I admitted that I was lost, undone, a sinner. I confessed to God that my dad was far more generous than I ever gave him credit for and that serving him at home would be far better than freedom in the far country. My father's goodness, not just my stupidity, led me to repentance. If I had only thought about myself, my hunger, my homesickness, and my loneliness, I would have surely died an agonizing death. The pain of my circumstances helped me to see my father in a whole new way. Hope was being born in me.

Here's the big question: If my father was so good to his servants and to my older brother, do you think, maybe, he would be willing to forgive me? I knew it was going to take a step of faith, but I also knew I had to get up, go, and ask for my father's forgiveness.

So, the journey began. Still far from home, little did I know that my dad had been waiting and watching, longing for my return. When he saw me walking in the distance, he ran to greet me and hug me. With shouts and celebration, my dad honored my homecoming by preparing a big feast and inviting the whole community to attend. My number-one priority was to confess to my father and ask for his forgiveness, but he interrupted me. He forgave me and the party began.

In the east, old men do not traditionally run, yet my father ran to greet me. The only reason I can figure is that the relationship a father desires with his son whom he loves will never allow him to sit still. But there is more. Being the wayward and prodigal son that I was, I had disgraced my family and the village. According to the laws of our land, I should have been put to death by stoning, but if anyone had tried it, they would have only hit my father with the stones that they threw because his embrace had me covered. I have since learned that is exactly what Jesus did for me on the cross.

RELATIONSHIPS ARE THE KEY

At home I discovered clothes, jewelry, friends, celebration, love, assurance, peace, and a bright future. I now wear a robe that my father has given me, no doubt his best, and a sonship ring that says I am His. That was my father's way of showing me and telling me that I no longer had to live as a slave, but that I was his child and everything that was his was mine.

If you have been in church for any length of time, I am sure that you have heard this story and know about this guy. It is a paraphrase of the story of the prodigal son, which is found in Luke 15:11-24.

The word *prodigal* means "wasteful." Yet, the story of the prodigal son is less about the mess the wasteful son made of his life and much more about the love and grace of his father. Did you notice that the father didn't chase after his son during his prodigal days? Rather, the goodness of the father drew his son back to his father, to a place of repentance and forgiveness.

Restoration

What I love about this story is that the father never gave up on his son, nor did he quit loving him. The son rebelled and went to the far country; I have been there. Haven't you? Regardless of how far we run, our heavenly Father always holds his relational position and his love never fades.

Eventually the time arrived that this son came to himself. You may be thinking, *Phil, what do you mean by this?* The prodigal son, like so many of us, thought that doing his own thing, regardless of what anyone else said, would bring satisfaction, freedom, and happiness. Then there comes a time when we are jolted back into reality and realize the heavenly Father's plans are far greater than ours. Repentance is realizing our wrong and turning back to head in the right direction. After the prodigal son came to himself, he then returned to the father.

One of the most amazing things about this relationship with our heavenly Father is that He is more than willing to wait on us to return home.

> The prodigal was lost.
>   – Jesus says, *I am the way.*

> The prodigal did some very stupid things.
>   – Jesus says, *I am truth.*

> The prodigal was dead in his sin.
>   – Jesus says, *I am the life.*

Each of us walk through this in one way or another. Many of us run from relationships while trying to find our own way, become exhausted, and then long for those relationships once again.

I remember back in the early '90s when I was fighting the disease of hyperaldosteronism, a disease in which the adrenal gland(s) make too much aldosterone. After going through a massive surgery for the removal of an adrenal gland, I was told that another surgery was possibly necessary. I sat in tears as I talked with Keli. I expressed to her that I waited my whole life to experience freedom from my parents and make my own decisions only to find myself longing to crawl back up in their laps and have them tell me what to do next.

Relationships

Relationships are the thing we most desire, yet we often run from them. Why? From the world's perspective, to need somebody is a sign of weakness. For a man to ask another man for help is emasculation in the worst sense of the word. Also, we lose trust when we have placed our trust in people, only to have them go and share everything we asked them to hold with great confidentiality. Sometimes it seems that life would be easier if we just left out the relationship component. However, we know that what is easy is not always what is best.

We were created for relationships. Primarily, we were made for a relationship with Jesus. Then we were made to be in relationships with others. Whether a child, a high school student, college student, single, married, middle-aged, or seasoned adult, we were all created for relationships.

Once I discovered my motivational gifts and put them to work in everyday life by serving others, I experienced the power of investing in others. One of the most valuable things I have learned in life is that investing in others brings far greater joy than self-indulgence and far more opportunities for relationships than spending all my time focused on myself.

The Reward of Investment

Several years ago, God opened the door of opportunity for Keli and me to serve as character coaches for the men's and women's basketball teams at Berry College in Rome, Georgia. This opportunity overwhelmed me with excitement as I draw energy from being with like-minded people. I didn't know much about basketball, but I loved sports, competition, and being with people. I was aware this opportunity to build relationships would cost us a great deal of time and energy. However, it would be a great investment for us personally and for the kingdom. Never in a million years would we have imagined what God was preparing to do in and through our investment at the collegiate level.

I discovered that relationships are built through the ministry of presence; so, in order to build and grow relationships, time must be spent with the people we wish to reach. Time spent while serving builds trust that creates and strengthens relationships.

Prior to this opportunity to serve Berry College athletics, we were reaching few college students at Northside. After this opportunity began, we have seen Bible studies launch with coaches, students, trainers, and student athletes. We have seen an atheist come to faith in Christ, and people who have been in church all their lives have surrendered to God. We see students serve in ministry and internships, not to mention people from all denominations grow as they (1) become unified in the essentials, things of top priority, (2) find freedom from the nonessentials, things of lesser priority, and (3) show unconditional love in all things. We have baptized students. We have students leading other students to Christ. We see more people who join hands and build community than at any other time in the life of our ministry. Sounds like the biblical description of the church, doesn't it?

Is it hard, taxing, exhausting work? Without a doubt.

Does it take a lot of time? Absolutely.

Is that what God has called us to? You betcha.

Does it bring about joy unspeakable? Certainly.

Does it bring God glory? Yes!

The relationships we have built are far more valuable to us than anything we could bring to them. These are relationships that will not just last for a lifetime but for an eternity. I long for these relationships. I need these relationships. We all are richer as a result of these relationships.

Time

If you are like most people whom I talk to about going all in with relationship-building, then you are probably asking yourself, when in the world will I have time? Great question! God has given every person the same amount of time: twenty-four hours a day, seven days a week. God also gave each person the power to choose how to use this time.

I shared with you in a previous chapter that my "life word" is *intentional.* My life verse is Matthew 6:33: *Seek first the kingdom of God and his righteousness and all these things shall be added unto you.* I also shared with you that my motivational gift is the gift of exhortation, teaching, and leading. This life verse, life word, and my purpose statement, which is "To develop godly leaders, encouraging them to live life beyond themselves," set my daily agenda. I believe with every fiber of my being that when we identify how God created us and surrender to the purpose for which He did so, we then become passionate about living out our purpose. Time is no longer as big an issue as I once found it to be. Do not get me wrong. My calendar is always full, and I often struggle to get it all in. However, the difference is my calendar is packed with building relationships while operating in my gifts.

Priorities

One of my greatest addictions in life has always been my addiction to busyness. While I understand that God is not impressed with our busyness, God had to bring me to a point in my life when I was forced to reexamine my priorities in life. Eventually I came to understand –

- God does not celebrate position titles or busyness.

- God longs for us to rest in our work, not just from our work.

- If we are ever going to close the loop of anxiety,

we must learn to build in margin for the things we
love to do and the things we were created to do.

God celebrates people who go to desperate measures to get to
know Him. For example, the fishermen who left their boats to
follow Jesus (Luke 5:1-11); the prostitute who faced embarrassment and shame to get past the religious leaders to the One she
knew would love her (John 8:2-11); the disciple who jumped out
of the boat to swim to Jesus (Matthew 14:22-33); friends who
destroyed a roof to get a crippled man to Jesus (Mark 2:1-5);
and a high-powered businessman who climbed a tree to get a
glimpse of Jesus (Luke 19:1-10).

Extraordinary things happen in an ordinary day when we
choose to do things God's way. People were and still are on the
top of God's priority list. He was, and still is, reachable. He was,
and still is, engaged in our everyday lives. He was, and still is,
prepared to meet our every need.

I began to understand that if relationships are more important to Jesus than religion, then relationships had to become a
priority in my life. If you look inside my journal, you will find
the following under the words "Daily Vision":

1. Stay personally connected to the Vine through
   prayer and the Word.

2. Be like Jesus.

3. Invest in my wife, children, grandchildren, staff,
   leadership, and the church.

4. Slow down and have fun.

5. Be intentional.

6. Stand in awe of God.

7. Stand fast to the orders of the Commander-in-
   Chief, Jesus.

8. Whatever I do, do it right. Be a man. Be a real man.

I suggest and encourage all of us to create space, manage our time, and take charge of our day. Otherwise, we will be at the mercy of it. The choice is ours. If people are God's priority, then we must surrender our agendas to mirror His agendas. So, if we will admit it, time for relationship-building really is not the issue. Making God's priority our priority is the bigger issue.

Relationships are the key, the secret sauce not only to this life but to the life hereafter. Awkwardness is often the only thing that stands between us and life-changing, life-enriching relationships. We must be willing to be vulnerable in our relationships. Sharing our weaknesses allows people to better relate to us as well as build bridges over which they may cross in their journey to everlasting life. May the legacy we leave be one of relationships with the Father and with the Father's children.

If you embrace the ones God puts in front of you, you will find that they will change your life more than you could ever change theirs. Be willing to intentionally seek to build relationships. Be willing to embrace those of a different color, culture, or generation, as they all have something beautiful to offer to you and God's kingdom.

Focus on the Present

Earlier this year, Keli and I were blessed with an all-expense-paid hiking trip to Israel. While on this trip we built some relationships that will forever enrich our lives, such as our relationship with an orthopedic surgeon, his wife, two teenage boys, and a young lady that the surgeon's wife was mentoring. After the second day, we had all become much more comfortable with each other. Our hiking in 100-degree weather for distances further than most of us were accustomed to trekking as well as walking in terrain fit only for mountain goats required us to reach out to each other for help and encouragement. It also inspired a willingness to cheer on these people we barely knew.

During this time the two teenage boys and I connected. Everywhere I turned, they were there. It was humorously noticeable. Being the old man who, out of pride, would not humble himself and say no to some of the climbs and tunnels, their pushing and cheering me on got me to the finish line. Without hesitation, I tell you that without these guys, I would have said no to several things on this hiking trip out of fear of heights and claustrophobia. They sure knew how to get the most out of this old guy.

One day, about three-quarters of the way through the tour, Keli asked the boys what they saw in me, the old guy, that would cause them to want to be around me all the time. The answer that came from their mouths said it all when it comes to the key on how to build relationships. They answered, "We want to be around him because he wants to be around us."

From the mouths of teenage boys came the common denominator of all mankind – the need to be needed and loved. Therefore, if relationships are the key, then letting people know that you authentically want them around is the key to building those relationships. Trust me when I tell you that it is worth the time and energy. Plus, you will be the greater benefactor.

Might you get hurt? Yep. Might you be rejected? Yep. Might you be sold out, talked about, and ridiculed? Yep. But do it anyway. That is what Jesus did. I cannot think of a better example to follow when it comes to being relational.

CHAPTER 7

CHURCH FOR THE UNCHURCHED

A noteworthy Sunday will forever stay etched in my mind. This was an exceptional day when bright, sunny skies shone on the warm smiles, shared energy, and power-filled worship of our congregation that must have produced a standing ovation from heaven. As our corporate worship time came to a close and the community of people made their way out our doors, I had the privilege of meeting a beautiful, African American lady who was visiting our church.

Her smile was radiant, her dress fashionable, and her head was topped with the finest of hats. This was not the first time that I had noticed her as her worship during our service was expressive and hidden from no one, though not the type that longed for all attention to be turned to her. Yet her worship was so authentic that anyone within view could not help but notice. With a quick greeting, a hug, and a "thank you for joining us in our worship service," we said our goodbyes and "hope to meet again."

Weeks turned into months of this lady's attending the church. After getting to know more about her, I discovered her passion was praise for Jesus. In one of our conversations, I asked her if she would consider joining our choir. At this invitation, her eyes lit up. She said for weeks she had dreamed of doing that very thing. From that day forward, this sweet lady with her smile, passion, and nice hat made her way to the choir loft with an energy like few I had ever seen.

For some, all we could see was pure, unadulterated worship, but for others, all they could see was a lady wearing a hat who seemed to be a little over-exuberant in her display of affection for Jesus. For those who felt this way, it was not long before they turned their judgmentalism into a form of a so-called prayer request. The news leaked out. With my personality, I seldom hear this kind of talk firsthand. However, this nonsense quickly made it back to me.

I must confess that, despite my love for Jesus and people, I wanted to choke some people. Come on now, do not read this like you do not know what I am talking about. There is not a pastor who has not on some occasion thought about laying hands on some of his people in a way that would satisfy his anger and frustration. Of course, I did not act on this impulse.

After several discussions with myself, I was certain I would stand in the pulpit and address this issue for the world to hear. But after much counsel with my wife Keli, I knew the Lord would not allow me to do so. You see, they did not know what they did not know because they had not taken the time to get to know this lady.

What I was privileged to know was that this precious woman had been in the Pentagon when the 9/11 attacks had taken place. She had survived traumatic injuries to her head that left a large hole in her skull, not to mention a hole in her heart from the loss of many colleagues who were not as fortunate. The hat was worn to hold the wig on her head that covered the hole. The smile and the exuberant worship were an expression of thanksgiving to the one true, living God, who not only saved her soul, but also had saved her life.

Short Sightedness

Too often we structure our churches in such a way that we only scratch the itch of people who look, dress, and act like us. By doing that, we structure the church in such a way that within seconds visitors would be certain that they were not welcome or would not want anything to do with this group called "a church." It would be no surprise to me if what I am telling you does not surprise you.

Not to linger long on the obvious or the negative, the questions we may need to ask are:

- What do we, as the church, need to do to reach the unchurched?

- What do we, as the church, need to stop doing to reach the unchurched?

First and foremost, we must stop focusing on ourselves. Our gathering as the church is not about us and our agendas. It is about:

- Worshipping corporately.

- Praying corporately.

- Making kingdom relationships.

- Equipping the saints to do the work of the ministry.

- Raising up disciples who will become disciple-makers, who will become disciple-makers.

- Doing life together.

- Taking the gospel of Jesus Christ to a lost world.

That is our purpose in learning and training. Many of us are raised with a plethora of information about the Bible, Jesus, and church, only to tuck it away while we wait on the return of Jesus. However, I believe the Jesus model is to equip others and multiply ourselves. We are to take the gospel of Jesus Christ across the street, to our workplaces, to our schools, to our circle of influence, around the world, and to our own families. I realize that the last one is the toughest because they know us the best.

If the church is going to be a healthy church that reaches the unchurched, it will be vitally important that we make discipleship a top priority.

> *Now the multitude of those who believed were of one heart and one soul; neither did anyone say that any of the things he possessed was his own, but they had all things in common.* (Acts 4:32)

Most churches in North American culture look nothing like the picture of the church in the previous passage from Acts 4. We are more closed off, to say the least. We spend much of our energy on defending our ideas of what the church should look like rather than discipling our flocks to reach people who have almost no concept of what a true Christ-follower looks like.

Proper Perspective

The highest priorities for the church of Jesus Christ should be to focus on our love relationship with Jesus, pursue relationships with others, and exemplify Jesus in our service to them. In doing this, the foundation will be laid and ears will be opened to hear the message of the good news of the gospel of Jesus Christ.

*For no other foundation can anyone lay
than that which is laid, which is Jesus Christ.*
(1 Corinthians 3:11)

There has to be a paradigm shift in our thinking from *going* to church to *being* the church. We are not employees and employers Monday through Saturday and then God-followers on Sunday. We are born-again God-followers 24/7 of every month and year. This creates our opportunities to deliver the greatest miracle known to mankind to experience, hear, understand, and embrace the love of the Creator God. That is what the lost, unchurched world is searching for. Yet, they will never even know it unless we become the church for the unchurched. When the broken know we love and care about them, they will not stonewall us when we tell our story of what Jesus has done for us.

With that understanding and great joy, I can say that at every church where we have had the privilege to serve, we have experienced:

- Unity

- Fellowship

- Peace

- Compassion

- Friendliness

- Growth, spiritual and numerical

- Accusations of not being typical or normal, which I love!

Now as awesome as this is, it is not where we settle in and get comfortable. For the church I am currently serving, our focus every day is to worship God, as well as to equip and launch saints for living life beyond ourselves.

Therefore, if anyone is in Christ, he is a new creation; old things have passed away; behold, all things have become new. Now all things are of God, who has reconciled us to Himself through Jesus Christ, and has given us the ministry of reconciliation, that is, that God was in Christ reconciling the world to Himself, not imputing their trespasses to them, and has committed to us the word of reconciliation. (2 Corinthians 5:17-19)

Being reconciled to Christ gives our ministry the power and authority to reconcile and lead the lost world to Christ. Is that awesome or what? This means we are doing life with the homeless, the drug addict, the prostitute, the doctor, and the lawyer. Yes, and empty seats will fill because relationships are being built via the glorious news of the gospel. Ordinary people will be doing extraordinary things because the church will get busy being what God has called us to be: disciples who are discipling disciple-makers who will multiply disciple-makers. This happens when we allow what we do vocationally to build a foundation to form relationships and friendships – when we live out our 24/7 ministry.

Broken

We all have experienced times in life when we have been so broken, hurting, and messed up that we could not even think of reaching out to the unchurched. We may be asking, *What do we do in times like these? How do we help the broken when we ourselves are broken?*

First, we must know that God does not necessarily cause sickness or brokenness, but God allows it.

Secondly, God does not waste the pain. He will use our brokenness, pain, and storms:

- To teach us how to depend on and trust in Him.

- To teach others from our experiences.

This means we must crucify our personal, immediate gratification in order to make a long-term kingdom investment in others. However, this is God's plan for us.

> *And we know that all things work together for good to those who love God, to those who are called according to His purpose.* (Romans 8:28)

Avoiding Isolation

How do we get the lost, unchurched people of this world from being broken, fallen, hurt, lonely and knowing no hope, no peace, and no purpose to experiencing peace, hope, purpose, redemption, and service to others? We do this by helping people understand we cannot do life alone. If we are to experience all that this life and the life after has to offer, we must be in relationship with others. We were not designed to be Lone Ranger Christians.

> *For in fact the body is not one member but many. If the foot should say, "Because I am not a hand, I am not of the body," is it therefore not of the body? And if the ear should say, "Because I am not an eye, I am not of the body," is it therefore not of the body? If the whole body were an eye where would be the hearing? If the whole were hearing, where would be the smelling? But now God has set the members, each one*

of them, in the body just as He pleased. And if they were all one member, where would the body be? But now indeed there are many members, yet one body. And the eye cannot say to the hand, "I have no need of you"; nor again the head to the feet, "I have no need of you." (1 Corinthians 12:14-21)

Every individual who is a part of the body of Christ must engage the lost to be a part of everyday Christian life. In this model we will find hope and support. I have a multitude of stories from my ministry where community from within the church made all the difference to those who were not engaged in the community. In other words, many stories show those who had no relationship with the church or Jesus, but because of one warrior of God – who dared to get out of the boat, lay aside his or her agenda, and pursue the lost, unchurched world – found a new purpose and meaning for living. Their hope grew, their faith changed, the expression on their faces changed, and their heart beat anew. This confirms the importance of the church in reaching the unchurched.

The Gospel

Before we can invite unchurched people into our Christian community, we must first understand how this community circle is formed.

- It is founded on the good news, the gospel of Jesus, the One who died for those who would reject Him, those who would curse and rebel against Him.

- It is the sacrifice that Jesus made for us on the cross that builds relationships of service rather than selfishness.

- It is selflessness and service that removes fear and pride.

- It is seeing every person through the eyes of Jesus rather than how the world might view them.

If we will strive to live this out through the power of the Holy Spirit, this lost, unchurched world will see the church like they have never seen her before. When this becomes who we are, the gospel we embrace will no longer be one we hope for, but one we walk in. We will understand that the gospel is good news – not something we do but something that has been done for us. It is the news of our being rescued. Rescued from what? *Wait for His Son from heaven, whom He raised from the dead, even Jesus who delivers us from the wrath to come* (1 Thessalonians 1:10).

Not only has He rescued us, He has chosen us to help others who need to be rescued. We have the privilege of bringing those who have never heard, who never experienced the love of God, along with us on this journey. God's using me to be a part of His rescue story in the lives of broken people has been one of the greatest joys of my life.

Look around. We are broken people in a broken world, which all stems from rebellion against a Holy God.

- Sin separates us from God.

- Sin separates us from one another.

- Sin alienates us from nature itself.

> *But God demonstrates His own love toward us, in that while we were still sinners, Christ died for us.* (Romans 5:8)

This truly is the good news! The Holy God from whom we have been separated by sin did not abandon us. He gave His only Son,

Jesus, to die for us to give us access to Him once again. No, we are not talking about a recovery program here; we are talking about a substitutionary work done on our behalf.

> *For by grace you have been saved through faith,*
> *and that not of yourselves; it is the gift of God, not*
> *of works, lest anyone should boast. For we are His*
> *workmanship, created in Christ Jesus for good works*
> *which God prepared beforehand that we should*
> *walk in them.* (Ephesians 2:8-10)

The bottom line is we were rescued by a loving God to be a body of believers – not individuals who function independently of each other – forming one body of Christ, equipped and engaged in sharing the good news to a lost, dark, hurting world.

> *The body is a unit, though it is made up of*
> *many parts; and though all its parts are many,*
> *they form one body … Now you are the body*
> *of Christ, and each one of you is a part of it.*
> (1 Corinthians 12:12, 27 NIV)

The common denominator among every person is their need to be loved. To receive the love of God, they must be rescued from the sin that separates them from His love. The only One who can save them is Jesus. But who will tell them? It is those God-warriors who will choose to stop doing church and start being the church.

Keys

What are some vital keys for the leadership to embrace to build a church for the unchurched?

1. Operate under the power of God's priority.

   But seek first the kingdom of God and His righteous-
   ness, and all these things shall be added to you.
   (Matthew 6:33)

2. Possess a passion for God and people.

   Jesus said to him, "You shall love the LORD your
   God with all your heart, with all your soul, and with
   all your mind." This is the first and great command-
   ment. And the second is like it: "You shall love your
   neighbor as yourself." (Matthew 22:37-39)

Bottom line: you can never love people more than you love God.
You should never use people to build ministry, but always use
the ministry to build people. May we stop expecting people to
look and act like us. Rather, embrace the way God uniquely
designs individuals.

3. Build relationships.

   A new commandment I give to you, that you love
   one another; as I have loved you, that you also
   love one another. By this all will know that you
   are My disciples, if you have love for one another.
   (John 13:34-35)

It is not what you have, it is who you know. Dare to get close to
people. Will you get hurt? Yes, but it is the Jesus model.

4. Focus on shepherding, not being a CEO.

   Therefore, take heed to yourselves and to all the

*flock, among which the Holy Spirit has made you
overseers, to shepherd the church of God which He
purchased with His own blood.* (Acts 20:28)

Yes, in many ways the church has to do business as an orga-
nization. However, may we never forget that we are an organ-
ism – the living, breathing bride of Christ. We must lead the
church by tending to her as a shepherd would his sheep, not
by pushing her.

5.   Pray for a healer's heart.

*I thank my God, making mention of you always in
my prayers, hearing of your love and faith which
you have toward the Lord Jesus and toward all the
saints, that the sharing of your faith may become
effective by the acknowledgment of every good thing
which is in you in Christ Jesus. For we have great
joy and consolation in your love, because the hearts
of the saints have been refreshed by you, brother.*
(Philemon 1:4-7)

It is vitally important to see every person with whom we come
in contact as a person in need of renewal – spiritual CPR.

6.   Learn to move past the past.

*Do not remember the former things, nor consider
the things of old. Behold, I will do a new thing, now
it shall spring forth; shall you not know it? I will
even make a road in the wilderness and rivers in the
desert.* (Isaiah 43:18-19)

Letting go of the past – forgiving ourselves and forgiving others – is key to all in the church getting over ourselves and on to serving the unchurched.

7. Encourage authenticity.

Confess your trespasses to one another, and pray for one another, that you may be healed. The effective, fervent prayer of a righteous man avails much. (James 5:16)

Share your weaknesses and your failures. Do not gloat in or dwell on weaknesses. However, if all we share are our strengths, we build walls over which others cannot climb. When we share our weaknesses, we build bridges over which others can cross to join us in authentic relationship. We must daily humble ourselves and be vulnerable. We must learn to say, "I am sorry."

8. Never preach an unobtainable gospel.

Preach the word! Be ready in season and out of season. Convince, rebuke, exhort, with all longsuffering and teaching. For the time will come when they will not endure sound doctrine, but according to their own desires, because they have itching ears, they will heap up for themselves teachers; and they will turn their ears away from the truth, and be turned aside to fables. But you be watchful in all things, endure afflictions, do the work of an evangelist, fulfill your ministry. (2 Timothy 4:2-5)

The gospel is within reach of all who will call upon the name of the Lord. Never use your platform as a weapon to attack or to look down on others. Most people already feel unworthy and unaccepted. We must deliver hope.

9. Refuse to sweep problems under the rug.

> *For the grace of God that brings salvation has appeared to all men, teaching us that, denying ungodliness and worldly lusts, we should live soberly, righteously, and godly in the present age, looking for the blessed hope and glorious appearing of our great God and Savior Jesus Christ, who gave Himself for us, that He might redeem us from every lawless deed and purify for Himself His own special people, zealous for good works. Speak these things, exhort, and rebuke with all authority. Let no one despise you.* (Titus 2:11-15)

Cancer breeds cancer. To delay our attention to cancerous matters is to destroy the church and her influence. We must deal with individuals one on one, and corporate issues must be dealt with corporately, but we must always remember to deal with all matters in love. I realize no one wakes up itching to deal with the problems of the day, but as warriors and followers of Christ, we must learn to deal with the elephant in the room. To refuse to do so is to put our leadership, and more importantly Christian influence, in question.

10. Admit you are not perfect.

> *Therefore, let him who thinks he stands take heed lest he fall.* (1 Corinthians 10:12)

The more humbly we walk, the more forgiving people are

towards us. The truth is that people do not think as highly of us as we think they do.

11. Surround yourself with people of strength in your areas of weakness.

As iron sharpens iron so one person sharpens another. (Proverbs 27:17 NIV)

I will say it again, it is not what you have, but it is who you know. Find good, honest, and trustworthy people who will dare to help make you the best version of you that you can be.

12. Model love.

But the end of all things is at hand; therefore, be serious and watchful in your prayers. And above all things have fervent love for one another, for "love will cover a multitude of sins." (1 Peter 4:7-8)

20/20 Vision

If I could encourage you in any way about being the church to the unchurched, I would say do not be afraid to embrace people. Model love by example. Do not get caught up trying to do a multitude of good things, simply become consumed with loving God and loving people. However, as a word of caution, do not allow people to become codependent on you. Always point them to Jesus.

My biggest struggle has always been busying myself as I search for the right program to meet the needs of people. However, a better program is not what people need. People simply need us to love them where they are and walk with them until God gets them to where He wants them. Our goal in life must be to love God and love people whether in the church or among the unchurched.

If you want your heart to beat the way God intended, then it is vital that you first answer this question: What is keeping me from embracing those within the church and those outside the church?

CHAPTER 8

IF YOU LOVE THEM,
THEY WILL COME

Some of the greatest years of my life and ministry were spent in Millington, Tennessee, in the late 1990s and early 2000. How we got there was amazing in and of itself. During my years with First Impression, there was never a time that I did not love what I was doing. However, I knew that God was preparing me for something else.

Our singing group had just finished a short tour in Africa and series of concerts in Central Florida. Exhausted, we arrived home late one Wednesday night. In my quiet time that Thursday, God pressed upon me the idea that my time on the road was over. To do what? I had no idea. One thing was certain, I could not escape that God was pointing me in a different direction.

The following morning a friend of mine, Rusty Reid, and I were standing on the number-one tee box of Stonebridge golf course in Rome, Georgia, when I asked Rusty to pray for me because I believed that God was calling me off the road. Rusty responded, "I believe you are deliriously tired, and I will not pray that."

After assuring him the physical fatigue had nothing to do with what I was asking him to pray, he agreed, but only with the stipulation that we would not talk about it anymore but simply enjoy a time of rest and relaxation on the golf course. I agreed. We prayed, and off we went. After many misdirected shots into people's yards, horrible putts, and lots of laughter, Rusty interrupted with a question, "Phil, if God is calling you off the road, what is keeping you from it?"

All I could tell him was that I had a great fear of disappointing my baby brother because thirteen years earlier we had made a promise to be in this for life. Rusty responded, "Then I will continue to pray." Our day went on without further discussion of this matter.

After arriving home early that evening, Keli and I were preparing to go to a life group party at the church when my phone rang. "Hey, Phil, this is Danny. What are you doing?"

"Getting ready to go to life group party. How about you?" I responded.

"I really need to talk to you. Can you have Keli go on to the party without you? I will come pick you up and then take you to join her after we finish talking." Danny said.

"That'll be great, man. Come on and get me," I replied.

After Danny arrived, we traveled only about a mile up the road before he pulled over into the parking lot of a softball complex. Danny then shared what was on his heart. "Phil, after arriving home from our last tour, I spent yesterday at a John Maxwell conference where I heard him make this specific comment: 'When two people with two different gifts are trying to operate on the same track, somebody is not maximizing their potential.' Phil, when John said that, I knew I had to sit down and talk with you."

"Danny, what is it that you are trying to say?" I asked.

"Phil, you know God is calling you to preach. As much

as I love your being in this group, you know that you are not maximizing your potential in what God called you to do," Danny explained.

On hearing this from him, I completely fell apart. As I tried to compose myself, Danny tried to comfort me with, "What is going on with you, man?"

After a few minutes' recovery, I had the privilege to share with my baby brother the story about my time on the golf course with Rusty and my fear of disappointing him (Danny). The beauty of this story is to know the very one I was afraid of disappointing came to me to be the encouragement that would launch me into my greatest years of ministry. After only a few more weeks on the road, I stepped aside to wait for God's open door to what was next for me, as well as for Danny and First Impression.

Mission Possible

Six months later, at our first ministry assignment, I met Larry Dagan, one of the greatest and kindest men I have ever met. Even his wife said that he was the greatest husband and father when she asked me to pray for him. My question to Ms. Leanne was, Why do I need to pray for him?

"Phil," she said, "I do not know if he has a personal relationship with Jesus."

For weeks that turned into months, I prayed for Larry.

Early one Wednesday morning Larry called and asked me if I could meet him. He was clearly upset. Without hesitation, I told him that I was on my way. After much conversation and Larry venting his frustration, he told me that regardless of how hard he tried to do things right, there seemed to always be something missing. I knew this was my open door to share the gospel with him and assure him that nothing else fills the void like Jesus, because He is always the perfect fit.

Later that evening, after riding around Millington, Tennessee, Larry Dagan bowed his head and his heart and professed Jesus Christ as his Lord and Savior.

I share this story to validate that relationships truly are the key. Living your life for something bigger than yourself will blaze a path that people want to travel. I had spent two years loving on Larry and Leanne's children, while Leanne and the kids attended church without their husband or father. This story illustrates that when we care more about building relationships with people than we do about building our resumes or churches, we create a winning team that will draw people who will want to know more.

Programs, fancy buildings, or the right kind of music are not what attracts the crowd. Rather, loving people the way Jesus loves people and for the reason Jesus loves people attracts people. Jesus loves people because He desires a relationship with them. He gave up the glories of heaven, allowed Himself to be separated from His Father, lived a human life with all its trials, and suffered a brutal death, only to conquer death by rising from the grave. He sacrificed His life because He loves us and desires a relationship with us. Through our personal relationship with Him, we can have a relationship with the Father.

Often, as pastors and shepherds, we do what we do for the wrong reasons. I have certainly been guilty myself. I refuse to believe that if we build it, they will come. I have seen millions upon millions of dollars spent on beautiful places of worship only for the new to wear off and the seats to become empty. I know what you are thinking right now: Hope you do not go off on a tirade about the church and all that is wrong with her. I promise not to do that. But I do want to offer what I believe the key is to a great ministry of reaching people with the gospel. I believe if we love them, they will come. This is what Jesus did. Without any partiality He gave His life for the world, knowing that many would reject him. We, too, must give our lives as we reach out to and serve all people, especially those who are broken, lonely, and paralyzed with fear.

> *My brethren, do not hold the faith of our Lord Jesus Christ, the Lord of glory, with partiality. For if there should come into your assembly a man with gold rings, in fine apparel, and there should also come in a poor man in filthy clothes, and you pay attention to the one wearing the fine clothes and say to him, "You sit here in a good place," and say to the poor man, "You stand there," or, "Sit here at my footstool," have you not shown partiality among yourselves, and become judges with evil thoughts? Listen, my beloved brethren: Has God not chosen the poor of this world to be rich in faith and heirs of the kingdom which He promised to those who love Him? But you have dishonored the poor man. Do not the rich oppress you and drag you into the courts? Do they not blaspheme that noble name by which you are called? If you really fulfill the royal law according to the Scripture, "You shall love your neighbor as yourself," you do well; but if you show partiality, you commit sin, and are convicted by the law as transgressors. For whoever shall keep the whole law, and yet stumble in one point, he is guilty of all. For He who said, 'Do not commit adultery,' also said, 'Do not murder.' Now if you do not commit adultery, but you do murder, you have become a transgressor of the law. So speak and so do as those who will be judged by the law of liberty. For judgment is without mercy to the one who has shown no mercy. Mercy triumphs over judgment. (James 2:1-13)*

People

Have you ever noticed that everywhere we look there are people? Regardless of where we go, it is hard to get away from them, and they seem to be the biggest problem in life. It has been said, "To dwell above with those we love, that will be a glory: but to dwell below with those we know, now that is another story."

For each of us, there are days that people get under our skin, drive us crazy, or push our buttons. But when we look through spiritual eyes, we do not just see crowds of people moving past or at us. We begin –

- To see unique individuals with their personal pain, each of whom is precious in God's eyes.

- To hear in their talk that they are not feeling loved.

- To see in their faces that they are paralyzed with fear.

- To notice their downcast gazes and slumped shoulders as signals of loneliness.

Having walked through these things myself, I may find it easier to spot some of these signs.

On the recovery side of fear, we recognize that fear is unhealthy, unreasonable, and unhelpful. It never accomplishes anything good. Lots of noise and lots of smoke, it takes us nowhere. Fear makes giant mountains out of little anthills and exaggerates things that may never come to pass. Fear is unhealthy, but unhealthy fears are learned behaviors that can be unlearned. But how will people learn if they have no one to teach them?

When we allow God to take our pain and make something good of it by using it to teach us about Him, we can share what we have learned with others. In turn, we will experience even greater freedom and victory in our lives. Then, because of the love we have shown them in their time of pain, they are drawn to us so we can point them to Christ. To love them is to share with them the real hope expressed by the psalmist:

The Lord is my shepherd; I shall not want. He makes me to lie down in green pastures; He leads me beside the still waters, He restores my soul; He leads me in the paths of righteousness for His namesake. Yea, though I walk through the valley of the shadow of death, I will fear no evil; for You are with me; Your rod and your staff, they comfort me. You prepare a table before me in the presence of my enemies; You anoint my head with oil; my cup runs over. Surely goodness and mercy shall follow me all the days of my life; and I will dwell in the house of the LORD forever. (Psalm 23)

Understanding the truths of this psalm is life changing.

1. When I understand that the Good Shepherd protects and defends me against my enemies, my clenched fists begin to open to receive the loving hand of God and the hands of those who try to help me.

2. When I understand the Good Shepherd leads His sheep when they do not know where to go, then suddenly the stress of trying to figure it all out eases because I become confident that He will give me direction.

3. When I understand that the Good Shepherd corrects any problem that comes along, the anxiety of not knowing what to do lightens.

To know this truth but not share it with those who are hurting is to refuse to love as Jesus loves. What a tragedy to leave people in their broken condition when we have the answer. To love people where they are and expect nothing in return will create an environment that most people cannot resist.

When I saw myself the way the Good Shepherd sees me, things began to change. Knowing this Shepherd provides food, shelter, and the necessities of life has provided great freedom from the fear and anxiety that dominated my life. Each day that I die to myself and live my life that way, I am also able to hear the voice the Good Shepherd saying, "I will provide for you. I will protect you. I will guide you. I will correct the problems in your life."

> *He will feed His flock like a shepherd; He will gather the lambs with His arms, and carry them in His bosom, and gently lead those who are with young.*
> (Isaiah 40:11)

Progression

What a promise! Way too awesome to keep ourselves. To know, understand, and experience the God of this universe supplying our spiritual, financial, relational, and health needs according to His riches in glory and fail to share it is disastrous! This should be the progression of faith:

1. We personally get to know Jesus.

2. We experience the good hand of His blessing and favor.

3. We listen to His command to take that with which He has blessed us and lavish it on those who have

never experienced His love, mercy, grace, and embrace.

With every fiber of my being, I believe Jesus is the prescription for the chaos of this world. How will they know unless someone tells them? How will they experience the love of Jesus unless someone shows them? God sent us His gift in Jesus. We are called to surrender with an all-in heart and attitude of sharing this gift with others.

Time to Move

I will never forget the season of my life when I wrestled with God's call to preach the gospel. After singing at a revival service in Augusta, Georgia, I was lying in bed and reading my Bible. I came to following text that made a huge impact on my thinking:

> *These are the words which Moses spoke to all Israel on this side of the Jordan in the wilderness, in the plain opposite Suph, between Paran, Tophel, Laban, Hazeroth, and Dizahab. It is eleven days' journey from Horeb by way of Mount Seir to Kadesh Barnea . . . On this side of the Jordan in the land of Moab, Moses began to explain this law, saying, "The LORD our God spoke to us in Horeb, saying: 'You have dwelt long enough at this mountain. Turn and take your journey, and go to the mountains of the Amorites, to all the neighboring places in the plain, in the mountains and in the lowland, in the South and on the seacoast, to the land of the Canaanites and to Lebanon, as far as the great river, the River Euphrates.'"* (Deuteronomy 1:1-2, 5-7)

This was the night when my world changed, the night that I heard God calling me to spend the rest of my life loving people the way Jesus loves them. Please, do not misunderstand me. It is obvious I am not Jesus and have fallen short of His standard much of my life. But my shortcomings have never minimized the calling God has placed on my life. As I read this biblical text, I heard the command that God had given to the children of Israel by Moses. They were to turn from the place where they lived and go to the land that they had already possessed. I struggled with the question: *Why is it that I am ignoring this command?*

The question we must ask: *Why is it we so often ignore the command when God says go?*

- Is it because we still wrestle with fear more than we want to admit?

- Are we uncomfortable with the situation facing us?

- Are we afraid people might think we are weird or crazy?

- Do we refuse to surrender and follow God because it is inconvenient?

- Is it that we just do not want to go?

Often while we try to follow the commands of Christ in this pagan world, we find ourselves in rather uncomfortable situations. People talk about us, make fun of us, and ridicule us. Sometimes even our own brothers and sisters in Christ do this. That one hits hard, doesn't it?

Sometimes we find that God's commands are inconvenient because they botch up our plans.

Lord, I just do not have time.

Lord, I do not even know them.

Lord, they are just not my kind of people.

There are also times we choose to flat out ignore His commands because we do not want to do it His way. I know. I get it. We love Jesus but surely there must be another way than the way He asks us to go about loving people. Then I am reminded of the time that Jesus withdrew a stone's throw away from his sidekicks and prayed, *Father, if it is Your will, take this cup away from Me; nevertheless not My will, but Yours be done* (Luke 22:42).

Yes, even Jesus wished there would have been another way to show the Father's love to the people. Aren't you thankful that Jesus did not let His will stand in the way of God's plan to save the world? If we are going to reach the world with the love of Jesus, we must not allow disobedience or our personal comfort zones keep us from fleshing out His plan and taking on our role in kingdom building.

The Road Map

As we continue in the passage in Deuteronomy, we read that when God told Moses and the Israelites to leave the territory of Moab, He gave them specific directions.

> "Break camp and advance into the hill country of
> the Amorites; go to all the neighboring peoples in the
> Arabah, in the mountains, in the western foothills,
> in the Negev and along the coast, to the land of
> the Canaanites and to Lebanon, as far as the great
> river, the Euphrates. See, I have given you this land.
> Go in and take possession of the land the LORD
> swore he would give to your fathers – to Abraham,
> Isaac and Jacob – and to their descendants after
> them." (Deuteronomy 1:7-8 NIV)

Take note: God even laid out the course for the children of Israel.

Have no doubt that our same God continues to direct us in our journey and our walk with Him. God gives us the roadmap to where He wants us to be and a plan for reaching those whom He wants us to bring with us on this kingdom journey.

What then is our response God? Too often we make excuses.

- I am willing to go God, but we need to talk about the direction you have given.
- God, it's just not detailed enough.
- I think I have a quicker or better route.

As I write this, I laugh at myself because of the numerous times I have tried to assemble something but refused to follow the instructions and in the end messing it up. Ultimately, I had to return to the instruction manual.

> *"For My thoughts are not your thoughts, nor are your ways My ways," says the LORD. "For as the heavens are higher than the earth, so are My ways higher than your ways, and My thoughts than your thoughts.* (Isaiah 55:8-9)

God's Word is our instruction manual to successful living and a roadmap to the promised land. His Word is the truth that not only will set us free but will bring hope and good news to a world of desperate people. As for me, if I set the course for my own life, it would without a doubt be the most self-centered agenda mankind has ever laid its eyes on.

When we choose to follow the playbook that fits God's design for our lives, we will walk in the fullness of His love, power, and might.

And my God shall supply all of your need

according to His riches in glory by Christ Jesus.
(Philippians 4:19)

God's riches are sufficient. Where He guides, He provides.

Notice what Moses went on to tell the people to do in preparation for his transferring his leadership:

> *"And I spoke to you at that time, saying: 'I alone am not able to bear you … How can I alone bear your problems and your burdens and your complaints? Choose wise understanding, and knowledgeable men from among your tribes, and I will make them heads over you.' And you answered me and said, 'The thing which you have told us to do is good.'"*
> (Deuteronomy 1:9, 12-14)

Moses told the children of Israel that their problems and burdens were too great for him to bear alone. He instructed them to choose wise and knowledgeable leaders.

As we apply Moses's directions to our lives, we too must find wise and proper counsel in our lives as we seek to obey God. As we would not take our cars to a lawn mower shop to be repaired, we must find those most qualified in our specific areas of need from whom to seek help – perhaps a pastor, Christian counselor, or true friend whom we can trust and who adds value to our life. The most qualifying factor for choosing this person should be whether his or her standard is the Word of God. How do you answer these questions?

- Who's your go-to person?

- Who is that cherished friend or person on whom you can count for godly, wise, counsel?

Let me encourage you to find one; ask God to lead you to the right person. Also, it is important to remember:

- Our ultimate counselor is the Lord himself.
- The Word of God is our standard.

Obedience

Moses spoke from his heart with warmth and encouragement as he instructed the Israelites to go forward and enter the promised land. His message is as personal to us today as it was to those whom he had been leading for forty years.

> *Look, the LORD your God has set the land before you; go up and possess it, as the LORD God of your fathers has spoken to you; do not fear or be discouraged. (Deuteronomy 1:21)*

When God says do not fear or be discouraged, let us trust that there is no need for us to fear or be discouraged. We can move forward in confidence.

I will never forget the day I asked Keli to marry me. With the ring in hand at the set location, I hit a knee and said "Keli, I love you. I want to know if you will marry me?"

"Phil, I like you, too," Keli responded.

The response that she gave me is not one that I expected. Okay, let me be honest – it was very embarrassing.

So, what is one to do at this point? Quit? Give up? Cave in to embarrassment, rejection, and humiliation? That might be some people's response, but it was not mine. I knew that I wanted this girl to be mine so badly that I was willing to face rejection again, if that is what it took. Oh yes, it ended well. We were married on April 18, 1981, and God continues to write our story to this day as we journey together.

When God says go, we often respond:

- "But God I am scared." To which God says, "I know you are, but remember I will catch you."

- "But God, I do not have the money." To which God says, "I know, but I have plenty."

- "But God, you know I cannot swim." To which God says, "I know, but I am your life preserver."

God is not just our comforter, counselor, or commander-in-chief, He is our good and faithful Father who will always hear and answer our cries. However, like Moses described the Israelites, we can rebel against God and not follow His leading in our lives.

Nevertheless you would not go up, but rebelled against the command of the LORD your God; and you complained in your tents, and said, "Because the LORD hates us, He has brought us out of the land of Egypt to deliver us into the hand of the Amorites, to destroy us. Where can we go up? Our brethren have discouraged our hearts, saying, 'The people are greater and taller than we; the cities are great and fortified up to heaven; moreover, we have seen the sons of the Anakim there.'

Then I said to you, "Do not be terrified, or afraid of them. The LORD your God, who goes before you, He will fight for you, according to all He did for you in Egypt before your eyes, and in the wilderness where you saw how the LORD your God carried you, as a man carries his son, in all the way that you went

*until you came to this place." Yet, for all that, you
did not believe the LORD your God, who went in
the way before you to search out a place for you to
pitch your tents, to show you the way you should
go, in the fire by night and in the cloud by day.*
(Deuteronomy 1:26-33)

Can you imagine the heart of God when He has done all that is
necessary, made the ultimate sacrifice, and all He gets in return
are disobedient, complaining children? Does that sound like
present-day, twenty-first century or what? As children of God,
we must embrace the fact that it is not about us, our agenda,
ideas, plans, or methods. It is about loving God, loving people,
and serving God by serving people. We must take the beautiful
gospel story of God's great love for us and lavish it on those who
do not yet believe. We must share how God not only delivered
the children of Israel but delivered humanity via the precious
blood of His Son, Jesus –

- from sin's captivity to the promised land,

- from everyday struggles to everyday promises, and

- from distrusting fear to a growing faith.

This whole chapter is devoted to the child of God who is willing
to leave the church culture, as we know it, for a kingdom culture
as God designed it. God's desire is a culture whose heart is to
leave no one behind, herald the gospel until the whole world
knows, and love people where they are. This kingdom culture
allows the Spirit of God and the good news of the gospel to
change the hearts of the lost and make an eternal impact on
the world.

Danger of Disobedience

But what if we refuse to be obedient to His command to go, love, and tell? Read carefully the words of Deuteronomy 1:34-35:

> *And the LORD heard the sound of your words, and was angry, and took an oath, saying, "Surely not one of these men of this evil generation shall see that good land of which I swore to give to your fathers."*

Because of their disobedience, many Israelites never entered the Promised Land. Their disobedience and rebellion resulted in discipline from God that kept them from receiving His blessings.

Likewise, today's child of God will not escape the consequence of his or her disobedience. Even more scary to me is the fact that many will never experience life's abundance because many who call themselves believers refuse to lay down their comfort and agendas to take that good news to those who do not yet know.

Please consider the question: What is keeping us from seeing the promises of the Lord fulfilled in our lives? I dare you to search for and discover the answer to that question as it pertains to your life. Your full potential as a believer rides on your willingness to answer this question and do something about it. The eternity of those who do not know about the love of Jesus or have never embraced the love of Jesus also rides on the willingness of each of us to answer this question.

I believe that it is vitally important that we love others the way that Jesus has called us to love them. In our doing so, many will embrace the greatest news ever.

Yes, if you love them, they will come.

CHAPTER 9

SERVICE VERSUS SURRENDER

The lesson of surrender can be one of the hardest but most important lessons we learn in life. For many of us, something has happened in our past that has caused us to become performance-based people, meaning we often feel the need to prove who we are versus our surrendering to whom God created us to be. The Word of God speaks of our need to surrender to Him and His plan for us. When we place our faith in Christ and His accomplished work on the cross, we become a new creation. This word *creation* comes from the root word *create*. It does not mean to change what already exists. Rather, it means to make something new out of nothing. When we surrender to God, He creates us to be someone brand new.

A problem for many of us is that we continue to hyper-focus on our past mistakes. We do this to the point of feeling like we need to prove ourselves to God and to others. This is no doubt a lie from Satan – a lie that brings about a self-effort that if not performed with perfection brings about guilt and shame. However, God never created us to "do" for Him, but to surrender to Him and allow Him to do through us what we cannot do for ourselves. All of this is done for His glory, not ours.

As children of the King, our Father calls us to be warriors facing our battles head on with a knowledge that it is He who fights our battles for us. When this paradigm shift occurs, we can live our lives on the offensive side of the ball rather than running from our past mistakes, seeing ourselves as failures, and buying into the feelings of unforgiveness and unacceptance. We no longer exhaust ourselves by overworking to prove ourselves worthy, trying to be somebody we are not, and fighting over things of no eternal significance.

A Warrior's Heart

It is vital that we live in Christ and become who we are meant to be. We must return to the life of the great adventure God has called us to live as men, women, husbands, wives, fathers, mothers, friends, leaders, and ambassadors of Christ. Too often we are guilty of living to impress each other and gain the favor of God. Yet, all the while, God has loved us with no strings attached. If we are ever going to fully embrace the warrior's heart that God intends for us to possess, then we must allow God to change our worldly perspective to a kingdom perspective. This will allow us to own our new-creation identity and regain what is rightfully ours.

My parents did an awesome job of leaving a spiritual inheritance for us boys. They taught us the Bible, set good examples most of the time, made sure that we knew the good news of the gospel, and invested in our spiritual well-being. I am sure some of you who are reading this book have also been blessed by having someone invest in your spiritual growth with an everlasting impact. If that is you, I encourage you to pick up the phone, call them right now, and thank them for their investment. You would be reinvesting back to them. If they are no longer living, then pause, thank God for their investment, and ask God to give you the boldness to pay it forward.

Beware: Satan is on the prowl to rob us of any progress we make. He seeks to do this through his lies, unfortunate circumstances, and feelings of unworthiness or rejection. If we do not take the proper steps in reclaiming our special inheritance, then we allow Satan to tempt us to say no to God's best for us. We unnecessarily will work ourselves to exhaustion in our vain attempts to claim what is already ours.

Leaving an Inheritance

Abraham left an inheritance for his sons: some very valuable water wells. In those days water was a valuable commodity that was much more guarded than we guard ours today.

> *Then Isaac sowed in that land and reaped in the same year a hundredfold; and the LORD blessed him. The man began to prosper, and continued prospering until he became very prosperous; for he had possessions of flocks and possessions of herds and a great number of servants. So, the Philistines envied him. Now the Philistines had stopped up all the wells which his father's servants had dug in the days of Abraham his father, and they had filled them with earth.* (Genesis 26:12-15)

Abraham's son Isaac obeyed God and harvested more than a hundred times what he had planted. His wealth continued to increase. As a result of Isaac's success, the Philistines became jealous and filled his wells with dirt to stop the water. They robbed Abraham's son of his inheritance. However, Isaac did not just sit back with his hands folded and allow the enemy to destroy what was his. He reclaimed, redug, and reopened the wells, which he was able to leave as an inheritance for his children.

That is exactly what we must do if our spiritual inheritance has been attacked by the Enemy. The only difference is that we must allow God to redig our wells for us, which only comes through our surrender to Him.

The light switch came on for me when I understood that I did not have it within me to fix all the wrongs, to reclaim all that had been stolen, or to put all the broken pieces back together. No, it would take One much greater than I to get this job done. His name is Jesus.

An inheritance is passed down for us to enjoy and then pass down to others. We have not worked for this; rather, a legacy has been left for us. This is much the same as what Jesus has done for us. He did the work of creation and redemption. Now it is our job to allow Him to live His legacy through us. It is not our job to reinvent the wheel, but to surrender to the journey. It is not working for Jesus; it is allowing Jesus to work through us. It is intimacy with Jesus.

I must confess I can become so busy in doing work for Him that I do not have time to spend with Him. My struggle is a prime example of service versus surrender. God says no to that way of living the Christian life.

Things That Matter

What kind of inheritance do we plan on leaving for our family? Houses, cars, businesses, jewelry, investments, or stocks and bonds? All this may be ok, but none of it will measure up in eternity. Is financial security important? Yes, but what will our family say at our memorial service if that is where our focus was? That he was a good man who worked hard, took us to church, and served his community? However, he was never at home. He was too busy serving everyone else, including the church, but never had enough time for us.

What is the most important inheritance anyone could ever leave? I believe this inheritance consists of deep wells of spiritual water that when consumed, the recipient will never thirst again. It is teaching our family and our circle of influence the importance of intimacy with Jesus – taking the time to sit next to Him and allow Him to love on us while we bask in His love. This was "a well" passed to me from my parents as an inheritance. It is one that I want to pass on to my children and grandchildren.

The Roaring Lion

At this point, I must issue a warning. Just as Isaac's inheritance was filled with dirt by his enemy, our Enemy is trying his dead-level best to eliminate our wells of their life-giving source. It is the very thing that can bring spiritual dehydration to the ones we love. When this temporary defeat occurs, it can bring paralysis to our faith walk. Our paralysis does not just affect us, but also affects those within our circle of influence.

Daily we face an Enemy who is far more cunning than the Philistines. He is a roaring lion roaming our land; he seeks whom he may devour and wants to fill our spiritual and physical wells with garbage. Why? Because he seeks destruction. How? He seeks to destroy us with spiritual discouragement and spiritual dehydration.

We must remember though: Jesus is the one who digs the wells in our lives and provides eternal water. Although Satan cannot take our wells, he certainly can fill them with the dirt of discouragement, doubt, and dehydration. Our job is not to dig another hole, but to rest in Jesus – the Living Water – who continuously digs and fills our wells.

> And Abimelech said to Isaac, "Go away from us, for you are much mightier than we." Then Isaac departed from there and pitched his tent in the Valley of Gerar and dwelt there. And Isaac dug again the wells of water which they had dug in the days of Abraham his father, for the Philistines had stopped them up after the death of Abraham. He called them by the names which his father had called them. (Genesis 26:16-18)

Notice that Isaac did not just go elsewhere and dig new wells. He reclaimed his inheritance and restored their names. He fought for what was his.

We must ask ourselves: Are we willing to forfeit our inheritance and walk away from what is ours? Or, are we willing to allow God to redig the wells that Satan, his demons, and the world has tried to stop up? Please, carefully consider your answers to these questions. We must be good stewards of the wells that have been passed down to us. We must maintain them, watch after them, and allow God to dig some new ones in each of our lives and fill these wells with His Living Water.

> Also Isaac's servants dug in the valley, and found a well of running water there. But the herdsmen of Gerar quarreled with Isaac's herdsmen, saying, "The water is ours." So, he called the name of the well Esek, because they quarreled with him. Then they dug another well, and they quarreled over that one also. So, he called its name Sitnah. And he moved from there and dug another well, and they did not quarrel over it. So,

he called its name Rehoboth, because he said, "For now the LORD has made room for us, and we shall be fruitful in the land." Then he went up from there to Beersheba. And the LORD appeared to him the same night and said, "I am the God of your father Abraham; do not fear, for I am with you. I will bless you and multiply your descendants for My servant Abraham's sake." So he built an altar there and called on the name of the LORD, and he pitched his tent there; and there Isaac's servants dug a well. (Genesis 26:19-25)

Isaac named his wells. The third well his men dug he named *Rehoboth*, which means "open spaces." He said he did this as *the LORD has made room for us, and we shall be fruitful in the land.* Our wells have names too. They are names like *joy*, *hope*, and *peace*.

Staking Our Claim

It is time that we stop working harder at what has already been done for us and start claiming our inheritance that has been handed down to us. It is time to reclaim what Satan has stolen from us and leave a legacy that points people to Jesus. We will not do this by doing more for God but by allowing God to do more through us for His glory. Jesus, the Living Water, applied the words of Jeremiah to himself:

> *The Spirit of the Lord GOD is upon Me,*
> *Because the LORD has anointed Me*
> *To preach good tidings to the poor;*
> *He has sent Me to heal the brokenhearted,*
> *To proclaim liberty to the captives,*
> *And the opening of the prison to those who are bound;*

To proclaim the acceptable year of the LORD,
And the day of vengeance of our God;
To comfort all who mourn,
To console those who mourn in Zion,
To give them beauty for ashes,
The oil of joy for mourning,
The garment of praise for the spirit of heaviness;
That they may be called trees of righteousness,
The planting of the LORD, that He may be glorified.
(Isaiah 61:1-3)

We will not inherit these wells by way of more service or activity. They will only come to us when we surrender completely to the One who dug the wells and gives the inheritance of eternal life – Jesus!

There Is Still Time

While we are still on the clock here on planet Earth, we have the opportunity to leave a legacy. Without equivocation, this legacy starts with Jesus and then is passed on to others. Apart from embracing the love that God has for each of us, it will be impossible to move from service to surrender.

- The Seven Wonders of the Ancient World were:
- The Great Pyramid of Giza, Egypt
- The Statue of Zeus at Olympia, Greece
- The Hanging Gardens of Babylon, Iraq
- The Mausoleum at Halicarnassus, Turkey
- The Temple of Artemis at Ephesus, Greece
- The Colossus of Rhodes, Greece
- The Lighthouse at Alexandria, Egypt

We have lost all or most of these ancient wonders. However, we have come up with lots of different wonders, including the seven wonders of the middle ages, seven natural wonders of the world, and seven modern wonders of the world. No doubt the greatest and only lasting wonder of all time is *God loves you*. He is crazy about you.

Every single person is of significance to God, but many people do not believe it. How could God really care about insignificant me? It is easy to believe that a Billy Graham kind of person would matter to God. However, we do not believe that our name would be on the list of who matters.

The fact is everyone matters to God. You and I matter to God. We all, even the most horrible criminals, matter to God. How could a thief, murderer, or rapist matter to God? We would not put their names on our lists of who would matter to God. The problem with our lists is they are all wrong. Why? Because everyone matters to God. Is it not for what criminals have done that they should suffer consequences of their actions? Yet, despite the crimes they have committed, they still matter to God.

Jesus had to deal with a group of people called the Pharisees, the religious elite of his day. The Pharisees had the opinion that God only cares about the good people. However, when we read God's Word, we discover that Jesus hung out with people who were on the wrong list according to the Pharisees. He spent his time with the non-religious, the rejects, the rebels, the undesirable, and the spiritually confused because these people mattered to Him. The Pharisees questioned Jesus about this as they did not believe that everyone matters to God.

> *Then all the tax collectors and the sinners drew near to Him to hear Him. And the Pharisees and scribes complained, saying, "This Man receives sinners and eats with them."* (Luke 15:1-2)

I imagine Jesus thought, *Guys, you ought to know better than this. I am here for the sinner's sake. The sick need the doctor not the well. So, where do you expect me to spend my time: with the sinners and outcast because God loves them or only with you who profess being God's chosen people?* Jesus got so irritated with them that he told three parables – earthly stories with heavenly meanings. Follow this unfolding story:

Parable Number One

Jesus tells the story of a man who lost one sheep. While he still had ninety-nine other sheep, the shepherd went to find the lost one. When he found the one, he brought it home. May I paraphrase for you what happened next? He threw a party because of the return of the one lost sheep!

> *So He spoke this parable to them, saying: "What man of you, having a hundred sheep, if he loses one of them, does not leave the ninety-nine in the wilderness, and go after the one which is lost until he finds it? And when he has found it, he lays it on his shoulders, rejoicing. And when he comes home, he calls together his friends and neighbors, saying to them, "Rejoice with me, for I have found my sheep which was lost!"* (Luke 15:3-6)

Parable Number Two

Jesus tells the story of a woman who lost one coin. While she still had nine other coins, the woman turns her house upside down to find the lost one. And when she found it, she threw a party!

Or what woman, having ten silver coins, if she loses
one coin, does not light a lamp, sweep the house,
and search carefully until she finds it? And when
she has found it, she calls her friends and neighbors
together, saying, "Rejoice with me, for I have found
the piece which I lost!" (Luke 15:8-9)

Parable Number Three

In this parable – the Parable of the Prodigal Son, which we discussed in a previous chapter – Jesus tells the story of a father
who lost one of his sons to selfish and rebellious behavior. While
he still had another son, the heart-broken father kept a vigil in
case the lost son returned home. Then, when the prodigal son
returned home, the elated father threw a party!

Then He [Jesus] said: "A certain man had two sons.
And the younger of them said to his father, 'Father,
give me the portion of goods that falls to me.' So, he
divided to them his livelihood. And not many days
after, the younger son gathered all together, jour-
neyed to a far country, and there wasted his posses-
sions with prodigal living. But when he had spent
all, there arose a severe famine in that land, and he
began to be in want. Then he went and joined him-
self to a citizen of that country, and he sent him into
his fields to feed swine. And he would gladly have
filled his stomach with the pods that the swine ate,
and no one gave him anything.

"But when he came to himself, he said, 'How many
of my father's hired servants have bread enough and

to spare, and I perish with hunger! I will arise and go to my father, and will say to him, "Father, I have sinned against heaven and before you, and I am no longer worthy to be called your son. Make me like one of your hired servants."'

"And he arose and came to his father. But when he was still a great way off, his father saw him and had compassion, and ran and fell on his neck and kissed him. And the son said to him, 'Father, I have sinned against heaven and in your sight, and am no longer worthy to be called your son.' But the father said to his servants, 'Bring out the best robe and put it on him, and put a ring on his hand and sandals on his feet. And bring the fatted calf here and kill it and let us eat and be merry.'" (Luke 15:11-23)

Party Time

What do these parables say to us today? They tell me that we need to be in the celebration business as there is reason to rejoice! Jesus says the discovery of one lost sheep, one lost coin, and one prodigal son is so overpowering that they had to have a party to rejoice. If this is true, how much more do we matter to God? I would say so much that we cannot even describe it. I believe that God's love is so perfectly pure and unbelievably limitless that it will endure our pleasure-seeking, self-centered lifestyles for years.

- God's perfect love for us moved Him to give us Jesus.

- Jesus's perfect love for His Father and for humanity moved Him to perfect obedience.

- Jesus's perfect obedience moved Him to suffer on the cross for the sins of the world. His love moved Him to remain on that cross until His final breath so that the job of redemption would be complete.

- God's perfect love through His omnipotent power raised His Son Jesus from the dead and seated Him at His right hand where Jesus sits today and intercedes on our behalf.

With all the work that God the Father and the Son did for us as well as all the work that the Holy Spirit continues to do through us, why should we feel a need to earn our heavenly Father's approval? I will tell you why.

- Satan attempts to pollute our wells and rob us of our inheritance.

- Satan attempts to busy our lives with works to earn that which we have already been given.

- Satan attempts to prioritize service over surrender in our lives because he knows the ruin it will bring.

Our service to the Lord must be an overflow of our intimacy with our Lord. May it be Jesus's working in us and through us. As my pastor and mentor Steve Drake once said, "I no longer see myself as a live wire energizing the world for Jesus, but simply a conduit through which the power of the Holy Spirit of God flows."

May our hyper-focus be surrender to our Father. With surrender comes freedom.

CHAPTER 10

TRUTH THAT DEMANDS ACTION

On a beautiful summer day in Ocala, Florida, I sat in my office preparing the message for the upcoming Sunday. The phone rang and my secretary informed me that Greggie McWhite was in the reception area and wanted to see me. Without hesitation, I invited Mr. Greggie into my office. Without a doubt, he is one of my favorite people whom God has allowed to cross my path. His sensitive and caring heart as well as a tender spirit would bring him to tears without much effort.

Mr. Greggie entered my office; he held an eight-inch piece of round fence post and a plastic turtle. I saw what he had and wondered if he was losing it. But shortly after he explained, and I was the one who was moved to tears.

"Phil, do you know how a turtle gets on a fence post?" Mr. Greggie asked.

"No, Mr. Greggie, I do not. Can you tell me?"

"Yes, Phil. The turtle only gets on the fence post if someone cares enough to pick him up and put him there," he explained.

"Mr. Greggie, I am not sure that I am following you."

"Phil, there are places in life that you and I can only get as the result of someone helping us get there. Your loving and teaching me from the Word of God has brought me to a place in my seventy-plus years that I have never been before. Thank you for helping me get where I could never get on my own."

This was a moment of great profundity – deep insight or wisdom that is transformational – which he had gained from his age, life experience, and spiritual growth. That day in my office, Mr. Greggie taught me a valuable lesson. We are not where we are as a result of our own doing. It is because someone has helped us get where we could not get on our own. It is when we embrace this fact with humility that we are ready to help others find their place on the fence post.

Total Trust

Where we once used to listen to the wrong voices, we have come to recognize the Father's voice after years of walking with Him. After years of missing the mark over and over, we have learned to fix our eyes on the One who can fix our problems. We have learned to trust the One who has our best interest at heart and can get us where we need to be headed in life.

> *Trust in the LORD with all your heart and lean*
> *not on your own understanding; in all your ways*
> *acknowledge Him, and He shall direct your paths.*
> (Proverbs 3:5-6)

Totally placing your trust and faith in God or in anyone or anything else takes a great amount of courage and risk. It is like asking someone to marry you or strapping on the pads for the biggest game of your life.

The reason most of us never undertake such great risk is what I believe to be the biggest dream-stopper in the world:

fear. However, if we believe the truth of God's Word, then it demands action despite our fear.

God has blessed me with loved ones who have been strong examples of how to live for Him and not give in to fear. Their consistent witness has provided living examples of what God can do through His children who put their trust in Him to do His work in and through them.

- My mother has lived her life in such a way as to provide a strong example of a woman who pushes beyond fear to live out God's plan for her life. I think about her trusting her heart to another man who became her husband and later my father. She knew that one day, death could take him before her. If so, she would have to face life alone without him. However, her love for him demanded action. So, she said, "I do."

- My oldest brother, Andy, who was paralyzed in a car wreck in his college years, faced the most difficult decisions one could face. Do you give up because your physical body will never be the same again, or do you choose to allow God to do in and through you what only He can supernaturally do? The biblical truth – *I do all things through Christ who strengthens me* demanded that he not give up (Philippians 4:13).

- My baby brother and his wife walked through the heartache of a miscarriage. They chose to walk in the truth that demanded continual faithful obedience despite their pain.

- My wife endured years of abuse, loneliness, and

pain. Yet, she continued to walk in obedience to God's truths.

- My children trusted that God would one day transform their daddy's life.

These amazing family members are heroes to me. They all have taken risks. They knew that the truth of God's Word demanded that they cross the Rubicon – the point of no return – in their faith walk with Jesus. They all continually leave their legacies in my life.

Question: Does the truth in which you have placed your faith demand action from you? Yes, it does! That action begins with:

1. Trusting God to do in and through you that which you cannot do on your own.

2. Knowing God will do through you what He has promised.

Action Thoughts

Please allow me to close this book and my story with a few truths that I have learned throughout my fifty-seven years.

- I am unique; there has never been anyone like me.

  o This uniqueness is not a virtue; it is a responsibility. While it is God's gift to me, it is to be my gift to God, for I was created to worship and serve God.

  o While I was created an original, I lived too long as a carbon copy of someone else, thereby living with a false identity.

  o God has not called us to be God, but to be ourselves.

- o I believe I am here for a reason. My purpose is greater than my challenges.

- I believed lies about myself.

  - o My true identity was buried beneath my mistakes and insecurities.

  - o I lived much of my life as another person for public consumption. I allowed others and myself to navigate my life, instead of being the man God created me to be and doing life His way.

  - o I became a stranger to myself in fear of not being accepted or viewed as good enough, which are lies from hell.

  - o I agonized in a performance-based life in fear of being a failure.

  - o I believed the lie I was told as a teenager: I would never amount to anything. However, the truth says that I am priceless in the eyes of God!

- We will never find ourselves until we find God.

  - o In digging deeper than my fallen nature, I can discover the nature of God in me. The sanctification process allows me to walk in His truth.

  - o The truth of God's love for me demands that I no longer live as a slave, but as a child of the King.

  - o The truth of God demands that I now rest in what Jesus did for me, not in what I can do for Him.

- o God's primary concern is not where we have been, but where we are going and Whose we are.

- Salvation is not the end goal; it is the new beginning

  - o As I live my life forward, I realize that God does it backward with the end in mind. God strategically places us in the right place at the right time in order to set us up for an unshakable destiny.

  - o Jesus did not die only to get me off the hook, but to resurrect the person I am destined to be.

  - o God takes our past circumstances and failures and uses them to prepare us for our future destiny. We can no longer live a life of regrets.

  - o To be like Jesus is my destiny in life.

- Learning continues through ministry.

  - o The deepest despair occurred when I pursued God's calling but did not feel worthy and couldn't forgive myself of past regrets.

  - o David's battle with Goliath was not won in the Valley of Elah with shield and sword, but on a hillside in Bethlehem as he protected sheep with a sling and a stone.

  - o Ministry is not about Phil's getting people to do the right thing. It's about Phil's becoming the right person and allowing God to do the right thing through him.

  - o Our current frustration becomes our future celebration if we continue to pursue God's best plan for our lives.

o If God ordains the dream, he will make a way.

o The most comforting psalms were written in the most uncomfortable situations.

o Too often I have allowed my circumstances to get between God and me.

o Nothing is more physically, emotionally, and relationally draining than trying to hold the planets in orbit.

o Self-confidence must die if holy confidence is to be experienced.

"Jesus does not offer to make bad people good, but to make dead people alive."[3]

Total Surrender

If truth demands action, then our action should be to allow God to do His work in and through us for His glory. If it is all about Jesus and not about us, then I would say it is more than all right for us to be the person God created us to be. Coach Don Meyer once said, "If you is who you ain't, then you ain't who you is." For me, I would rather be hated for who I am than loved for who I am not. The grace of God offers atonement that covers our shame, so we do not have to cover ourselves with fig leaves.[4]

Let's not die until we are dead. Let's not live by what we see but by faith in God's Word and His promises. Let's slow down to gain traction and save energy by minimizing wasted motion. Let's stop trying to manufacture fruit but start bearing the fruit that God produces through us instead.[5]

3   Ravi Zacharias, *The Grand Weaver: How God Shapes Us Through the Events of Our Lives* (Zondervan: 2007).
4   Reference to Genesis 3:21.
5   Reference to Galatians 5:22-23.

In living out the words *In God We Trust*, it is vital to remember the depth of our spiritual health is dependent upon our willingness to surrender to God. He is the only One who can make us whole.

Oh yes, one last thing, if we really want to live, then it is vital that we first die.

I have been crucified with Christ; it is no longer I
who live, but Christ lives in me; and the life which
I now live in the flesh I live by the faith in the Son
of God, who loved me and gave Himself for me.
(Galatians 2:20)

ACKNOWLEDGEMENTS

We want to say special thanks to:

Debbie Rasure

Sandy Campbell

Rick Coram

Pattie Luther

Steve Drake

Kris and Robin Den Bestin

Bill and Amanda Wiley

Richard and Gail Cordero

Rodney and Robbie Wilson

Phyllis Bynum

Thank you for your endless hours of proofing/editing and listening to my ideas. We could not have done this without your labor of love and financial sacrifice.

ABOUT THE AUTHOR

P hil Wade is a husband, father, grandfather, pastor, character coach, author, and founder of Vital Signs Ministry. Phil trusted Christ to be his Savior on October 25, 1991, and after thirteen years of singing with the contemporary Christian country trio, First Impression, he surrendered to pastoring the local church. His passion is to preach God's Word, pastor the church, and encourage leaders to live life beyond themselves.

Phil enjoys ministering to pastors, churches, leaders, students, corporate America, nationally and abroad by the way of:

- Character coaching
- Church revitalization
- Pastoral care

- Staff coaching
- Leadership training (corporate and church)
- Conference speaking
- Men's wild game dinners
- Marriage retreats, with his wife, Keli
- Revivals

Phil's greatest desire is to see people come to faith in Christ and live their lives in a spiritually healthy way by maximizing their potential for the glory of God.

www.philwade.net

CONNECT WITH US...

For additional copies of this book,
daily "Vital Signs" devotionals,
or to contact the authors,
go to **www.philwade.net**
or **facebook.com/philwadenet**

Other Similar Titles

Following Christ,
by Charles H. Spurgeon

You cannot have Christ if you will not serve Him. If you take Christ, you must take Him in all His qualities. You must not simply take Him as a Friend, but you must also take Him as your Master. If you are to become His disciple, you must also become His servant. God-forbid that anyone fights against that truth. It is certainly one of our greatest delights on earth to serve our Lord, and this is to be our joyful vocation even in heaven itself: His servants shall serve Him: and they shall see His face (Revelation 22:3-4).

Charles H. Spurgeon originally wrote this book for members of the Young People's Society of Christian Endeavor. Spurgeon's heartfelt writing style makes this book one that today still encourages believers to move into Christian action. He emphasizes simply moving forward, using the talents and resources you already have at your disposal, for the Lord's service and your own eternal reward. The concepts presented are easy to understand and straight-forward, if only you are ready to lay down your life to follow Christ.

Available where books are sold.

A Word to Fellow Pastors and Other Christian Leaders, by Horatius Bonar

The objective of the Christian ministry is to convert sinners and to edify the body of Christ. No faithful minister can possibly rest short of this. Applause, fame, popularity, honor, and wealth – all these are vain. If souls are not won, and if saints are not matured, our ministry itself is futile.

Questions we have to ask ourselves: Has it been the purpose of my ministry and the desire of my heart to save the lost and guide the saved? Is this my aim in every sermon I preach and in every visit I make? Do I pray and toil and fast and weep for this? Do I spend and am I spent for this, counting it, next to the salvation of my own soul, my greatest joy to be the instrument of saving others? Have I seen the pleasure of the Lord prospering in my hand? Have I seen souls converted under my ministry? Have God's people found refreshment from my lips and gone on their way rejoicing, or have I seen no fruit of my labors? Am I content to remain fruitless? Am I satisfied to preach without knowing of one saving impression I made or one sinner awakened?

Available where books are sold.

Prevailing Prayer,
by Dwight L. Moody

This book is a comprehensive study on the subject of prayer, and will show you that there are nine elements which are essential to true prayer. These elements are as follows: Adoration, Confession, Restitution, Thanksgiving, Forgiveness, Unity, Faith, Petition, and Submission.

Dwight Moody expounds on these nine elements in this volume, using illustrations and stories to validate what he is saying and to help make the truths in this book stick.

Available where books are sold.

The Soul Winner,
by Charles H. Spurgeon

As Christians, our main business is to win souls. But, in Spurgeon's own words, "like shoeing-smiths, we need to know a great many things. Just as the smith must know about horses and how to make shoes for them, so we must know about souls and how to win them for Christ." Learn about souls, and how to win them, from one of the most acclaimed soul winners of all time.

Available where books are sold.